KIDS
As Planners

A Guide to Strengthening Students, Schools and Communities through Service-Learning

Revised and Expanded Third Edition

A Note Concerning Copyright

KIDS Consortium Contributing Writers .... Michael Blankenburg, Education Consultant
Barbara Fiore, Education Consultant
Jo Gates, AmeriCorps*VISTA
Tracy Harkins, Education Programs Manager
Matthew Robinson, Education Consultant
Fran Rudoff, Executive Director

Writer/Editor: .... Marina Schauffler, Natural Choices, LLC
http://www.naturalchoices.com/

Design: .... Jeff Soifer, Encompass Marketing & Design
http://www.encompassmarketing.com/

Printer: .... Penmor Lithographers, Lewiston, Maine

Photos: .... KIDS Consortium would like to thank all the
generous teachers, students and others who
kindly contributed photographs to this book.

Acknowledgments

We are extremely grateful to all of the service-learning coordinators, educators, students and community leaders who have worked with the Consortium over the past decade to implement and refine the KIDS service-learning model. Their collective experience, wisdom and vision have helped shape the tools and approaches described in this guide.

Valuable contributions, reviews and advice were provided for this and earlier editions by:

Steve Brown, Lisbon Central School, Lisbon, Connecticut

Connie Carter, Operation Breaking Stereotypes, Orono, Maine

Maureen Charron-Shea, Harwood Union High School, South Duxbury, Vermont

Mary Concannon, Former Program Associate, KIDS Consortium

Christel Driscoll, Lincoln Middle School, Portland, Maine

Tina Clark Edwards, Consulting Educator and Trainer, Freeport, Maine

Linda Freese, Poland Regional High School, Poland, Maine

Joanne Harriman, Mount Desert Island Regional School System, Mount Desert, Maine

Amy Hediger, Poland Community School, Maine

Barbara Kaufman, Former Education Consultant, KIDS Consortium

Melissa London, Heath School, Brookline, Massachusetts

Susan Martin, Lewiston Public Schools, Lewiston, Maine

Matt McLane, Montpelier High School, Montpelier, Vermont

Heidi McGinley, Formerly with Maine Department of Education

Donna Oliver, Eddington Elementary School, Eddington, Maine

Alice Olsen, Winthrop Elementary School, Winthrop, Maine

Dan Porter, IW Financial, Portland, Maine

Pam Rolfe, Maine Department of Education

Marvin Rosenblum, Founder, KIDS Consortium

Melissa Skahan, Former Service-Learning Coordinator, Maine School Administrative District 51

Sarah Simmonds, Cape Elizabeth School Department

Trisha Smith, Bangor Middle School, Bangor, Maine

Maryli Tiemann, Educator, Brunswick, Maine

Aaron Townsend, Former Middle School Teacher, Auburn, Maine

William "Bumper" White, University of Southern Maine, Lewiston-Auburn College

Terri Marin from KIDS Consortium collected photographs, quotes and resources for this revised edition of KIDS as Planners.

We wish to acknowledge funders of both KIDS Consortium and the school districts described in this publication: Center for Civic Education, Davis Conservation and Family Foundations, Horizon Foundation, L.L. Bean Inc., Maine Juvenile Justice Advisory Group, Maine Community Foundation, Maine Office of Substance Abuse, Poland Spring Water Company, Sam L. Cohen Foundation, Simmons Foundation, State Farm Companies Foundation, Surdna Foundation, UNUM Foundation, US Environmental Protection Agency, and the Corporation for National Service under Learn and Serve America, Grants No. 94LSGME003, 97LSFME304, 00LCGME048, 03KCHME002, 06KSHME001, and 09KSAME002.

Major support for the first edition of this guide was provided by funds from the W.K. Kellogg Foundation through the Maine Department of Education, as part of Learning in Deed—a national initiative to expand the use of service-learning in K-12 classrooms.

Opinions or points of view expressed in this document are those of Consortium staff and do not necessarily reflect the official position of these funders.

Foreword

Having worked as a teacher for decades, in many varied settings and roles, I know how difficult a calling it can be. Those teaching today, who face a parade of new demands, add-ons and administrative fiats, must find it especially frustrating and exhausting.

What lightened my load as a teacher was discovering that I could work alongside my students, inviting them as partners in the learning process. It reenergized me to see kids excited about school, actively engaged in mastering a subject, and committed to make a difference in their communities. The skills they developed in this process—like critical thinking, problem-solving, and teamwork—would serve them well throughout life. They were learning far more than a set curriculum: they were becoming effective citizen leaders.

Since I founded KIDS (Kids Involved in Doing Service-Learning) Consortium almost two decades ago, the value of this engaged, experiential approach to education has been reaffirmed through extensive research and—more importantly—through the lives of countless students across the nation. KIDS is now at the forefront of service-learning, one of the most promising educational strategies.

This edition, the third since the *KIDS as Planners* guide was first published in 2000, incorporates new tools and techniques, inspiring stories and updated guidance. This guide is not an add-on, compounding the relentless demands you already face. Rather the KIDS model supplements your skills with the boundless energy and creativity of youth. It helps you forge authentic partnerships linking your school and students to the larger community.

From the very first, KIDS Consortium has emphasized collaboration—within and beyond the classroom. We look forward to working with you as you explore the limitless potential of service-learning and discover how it can revitalize your teaching, your school and your community.

Marvin Rosenblum
Founder and Past President
KIDS Consortium

Table of Contents

Chapter 1:
KIDS and Service-Learning

Reflection   Collaborative Environment   Public Relations   Celebration   Curriculum, Instruction and Assessment

Define Service-Learning   Discover Needs/Problems   Investigate Problems   Research Solutions   Decide on a Project   Plan the Project   Implement the Plan   Evaluate

Case Study: Collecting Electronic Waste

While studying the Law of Conservation of Matter and Energy, eighth-grade students at Lincoln Middle School in Portland, Maine watched several Internet videos and saw images of electronic waste (e-waste) pollution in China, India and several African countries. They learned about different types of e-waste on the Internet and a guest speaker from a regional, nonprofit waste management firm told students about the problems associated with e-waste and why this form of waste generally can't be disposed of in traditional facilities. Students did further individual research into the economics of e-waste and its health and environmental effects.

To gain a better understanding of how significant the e-waste problem was locally, students completed an online survey documenting the amounts and types of e-waste in their own homes. In math class, students analyzed the data and were shocked to discover the volume of e-waste that had accumulated in their homes. Based on the number of households in Portland, they estimated how much e-waste might be in households citywide.

All 65 eighth-graders then gathered to discuss what could be done. They identified two needs their project would address: informing local residents about the hazards of e-waste and the need for proper disposal; and helping get the waste out of their homes. Students worked in small groups to generate possible solutions, and concluded that most of their ideas fit within three proposed strategies: 1) hosting an e-waste collection booth at a school carnival; 2) doing a neighborhood e-waste pickup drive; and 3) developing public service announcements and flyers to inform the community about proper e-waste disposal.

Students broke into working groups based on their interests and, over two weeks, did further Internet research and interviews to develop a detailed task list. As they began implementing their projects, they tracked progress and next steps through daily journal entries.

Students shared news of their project with the school through daily announcements and periodic flyers as well as postings on the school's website. They reminded parents about collection dates through an automated phone call they prepared themselves (with school approval). Students did a community "walkabout" to inform neighbors of the collection dates and drop off flyers.

Students got so enthusiastic about the project they began taking extra initiatives on the weekends to advance the project goals. They also talked about the project with their parents—who shared news of it with coworkers, extended family and colleagues. Students contacted radio and television stations in order to recruit more community participants and they succeeded in getting a live radio interview, brief television story, and letter to the editor.

At the two collection events (held in cooperation with Portland Public Services), community residents brought enough e-waste (2,627 electronic items) to fill a 26-foot box truck. Students tracked the types of e-waste collected, analyzing and discussing the results afterward. Students also completed a follow-up online survey of their households, which indicated that people would handle their future disposal of e-waste far more responsibly than in the past.

What Is Service-Learning?

Service-learning is a teaching strategy that empowers youth as they work with community partners, applying academic knowledge and skills to address real problems and needs. Through service-learning, young people gain essential problem-solving, communication and teamwork skills that help them succeed as engaged students, civic volunteers, future employees, and entrepreneurs. "Service-learning" is sometimes confused with "community service" or "community-based learning." While all three educational approaches engage local people and places, they are distinct (see sidebar on these terms). Service-learning extends far beyond traditional community service (in which students work voluntarily on beneficial projects), incorporating a strong academic component that links the service experience to curricular objectives.

Service-learning puts students at the center of problem-solving: here students work with a community expert to determine the health of a local stream.

Commonly Confused Terms— Definitions and Examples

Community-based Learning:

An approach that enhances the curriculum by using community members and places as resources for learning.

A teacher decides to center a unit of ecology on a stream near the school. Students visit the site frequently, collecting water samples and identifying plants and animals.

Community Service:

An activity that engages people in addressing needs of their schools and communities.

Twice a year, students take a field trip to collect trash and recyclables along the banks of a local stream.

Service-Learning:

A method of teaching and learning that challenges students to identify, research, propose and implement solutions to real needs in their school or community as part of their curriculum.

When students discover that a local stream is degraded, their class collaborates with an environmental group to design a plan of action that addresses stream pollution and aligns with the school's curriculum. Students conduct water-quality tests and research possible contamination sources. They analyze data and present their findings and solutions to the environmental group, which uses this information to improve watershed protection.

KIDS Service-Learning Model

Students apply their academic knowledge and skills to solve community concerns through the KIDS (Kids Involved in Doing Service-Learning) approach to service-learning. This award-winning model fosters authentic student learning that provides young people with critical skills for the 21st century. Students gain knowledge, not simply from teachers, but through a guided interaction with their environment. Immersion in a KIDS service-learning project builds academic skills, strengthens student resilience, and deepens commitment to civic participation.

The KIDS service-learning model encourages students, teachers and administrators to take on new roles. Students become partners with teachers and community members. Teachers act as coaches and facilitators and often team up with colleagues, working cooperatively to integrate projects into their curriculum. Administrators open doors so that students can collaborate with community partners, addressing concerns beyond the school grounds.

Three key principles are the foundational legs underlying the KIDS service-learning model: academic integrity, apprentice citizenship, and student ownership. These elements should be central to every service-learning project. As you progress through this guide, learning more about steps and standards that will enhance your project, continue to rely on these core principles as a litmus test of project success. A summary of the KIDS principles can be found in the Appendix on page 94

Academic Integrity

Service-learning projects grow out of community needs but are an integral part of the curriculum. Educators (whether in-school classroom teachers or after-school/ summer program leaders) are busy with existing demands, and cannot afford to take on "yet another thing to teach." Service-learning offers an effective instructional strategy that helps students meet state learning standards and achieve measurable outcomes while fostering meaningful experiences for both students and teachers. By linking service-learning projects to curricular objectives, teachers play an important facilitation role, actively helping students connect their community experiences with lasting academic learning.

Key Elements of Academic Integrity

▶ **Integrated:** integral part of the academic program

▶ **All Learners:** meets the needs of all students

▶ **Facilitated:** teachers play an important facilitation role

▶ **Learning and Assessment:** students apply and demonstrate new knowledge and critical skills

▶ **Relevant:** school is relevant and students are motivated to learn

KIDS as Planners

Projects involving "real life" concerns can motivate students at all levels, engaging those who don't respond well to traditional classroom approaches and encouraging high-ability students to reach beyond the set curricula. By giving diverse students' opportunities for growth and expression, service-learning helps them apply and demonstrate new knowledge.

The Learning Pyramid:
Average Retention Rates for Different Teaching Methods

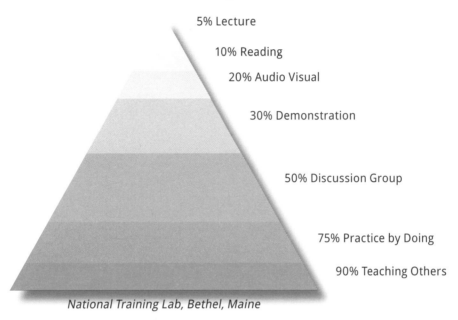

5% Lecture

10% Reading

20% Audio Visual

30% Demonstration

50% Discussion Group

75% Practice by Doing

90% Teaching Others

National Training Lab, Bethel, Maine

Schools typically emphasize linguistic and logical-mathematical intelligences, but many educators are working to teach in more active and experiential ways that support other forms of intelligence. Research shows that some of the most common instructional strategies—such as lectures and reading—are the least effective at promoting long-term learning. According to the National Training Lab (see pyramid diagram), students typically retain knowledge best when actively engaged in discussion, practicing new skills, and teaching others. Service-learning often includes these experiential approaches, drawing on what psychologist Howard Gardner terms "multiple intelligences"—the diversity of ways that people solve problems and express their creativity (see Gardner's book *Multiple Intelligences* or Thomas Armstrong's *Multiple Intelligences in the Classroom—3rd edition*).

> "Creativity is as important in education as literacy and we should treat it with the same status."
>
> — *Sir Ken Robinson, international creativity expert, 2006*

Building Skills for the 21st Century

Many educators and parents seek better ways to prepare students for the interconnected, complex and competitive world in which they will work—where individuals may have many different jobs and even several careers over their lifetimes. Students need to be active, creative participants in a dynamic arena driven by rapidly evolving innovations and knowledge. They need to know how to manage, interpret and act on the torrents of information they'll encounter; work and communicate effectively with diverse people; and tackle complex, interdisciplinary work.

A growing number of educational reform efforts emphasize the development of "21st Century Skills" through learning approaches that are "student-centered," "personalized," and/or "problem-based." As the Partnership for 21st Century Skills (www.21stcenturyskills.org) observes, students need skills that will "withstand the test of time, fluctuations in the economy and the marketplace, and dynamic employment demands." The KIDS service-learning model supports these reform efforts by helping students develop skills that are increasingly critical to their own and the world's future. These include the ability to:

- ▶ solve complex, multidisciplinary problems;
- ▶ think critically, analyze information and make well-informed choices;
- ▶ be creative and entrepreneurial;
- ▶ communicate effectively in person and in writing;
- ▶ collaborate and foster teamwork;
- ▶ participate in civic life and democratic decision-making; and
- ▶ cultivate an ongoing commitment to learning.

> "The benefits of quality service-learning experiences are tightly connected to the development of twenty-first century skills—critical thinking, communication, problem solving, and collaboration. Collaboration is a particular strength of the KIDS method. In service-learning, students are all working together to solve common problems. We seldom do that in public education, and it's a powerful thing."
>
> – *Rob Liebow, Superintendent, Mount Desert Island Regional School System*

Apprentice Citizenship

One of the critical skills students need for the 21st century (see sidebar) is civic literacy or apprentice citizenship, learning how to effectively participate in and constructively contribute to their communities. The KIDS service-learning model views young people as vital community members who can apply their knowledge, skills and energy to local, regional and global concerns. Students develop expertise in community issues by working closely with local experts, organizations and government agencies.

By collaborating with authentic partners on real problems, students develop civic awareness and skills needed for effective citizenship, such as critical thinking, problem-solving, cooperation and advocacy. Community members value the work that students do because it meets genuine needs. This partnership, as author Frances Moore Lappé observes (see sidebar), helps build "a new culture of democracy" in which students, teachers and community partners are "learning and teaching the arts of decision-making, active listening, negotiation, mediation, and evaluation." Development of these skills enriches both individual students and their communities: those involved in KIDS projects report a greater sense of belonging and commitment to their community.

Key Elements of APPrentice Citizenship (Problem + Partner(s))

▶ **Belonging:** students feel as though they belong to a community

▶ **Authenticity:** students' work is valued because it meets real community needs

▶ **Community Expertise:** students learn with and from community members

▶ **Civic Awareness:** students become effective citizens

"Ideally, we want students to become clear and effective communicators, self-directed and life-long learners, creative and practical problem-solvers, responsible and involved citizens, collaborative and quality workers, and integrative and informed thinkers. Service-learning allows students to apply these guiding principles. My students didn't do service-learning projects for the grade, although they were graded on various tasks throughout. They did them because they were great projects in which they were invested. They were engaged in a collaborative effort that mattered to others and truly made a difference! Every human being needs to feel valued, and I've experienced how that can happen through service-learning."

— *Trisha Smith, teacher, William S. Cohen School, Bangor, Maine*

Revitalizing Democracy by Frances Moore Lappé

I believe our democracy is now taking its first wobbly steps in a profound historical transition, and whether we learn to walk this new path with grace depends in large measure on the creativity and courage of our teachers.

In millions of ways, our culture bombards us with debilitating messages denying our role in shaping our own future. For example:

▶ Public life is what someone else—a celebrity or big shot—has.

▶ If I'm not a celebrity, public life is unappealing and unrewarding. It's all about ugly conflict.

▶ Public life competes with—even distracts from—a satisfying private life and that's where the real rewards of life are.

▶ My only job as a citizen is to vote; then I can sit back and blame the corrupt and the incompetent.

Each of these myths represents an obstacle to creating a truly functional democracy. What can be done? Fortunately, millions of Americans are asking that question. Their answers help seed the emergence of a new culture in which democracy is not something we have but what we "do," a way of life that involves us daily—not just at the ballot box, but in the classroom, community and workplace.

The KIDS model demonstrates that "doing democracy" is a learned art. And like any skill in life—from reading to basketball to knitting—we enjoy it more as we learn to do it better. So as you attend with your students to learning and teaching the arts of decision-making, active listening, negotiation, mediation, and evaluation, you are building a new culture of democracy. From our observations, once youngsters learn these arts, and the associated habits of mind and heart, you can't put that genie back in the bottle. Their lives are enriched forever as they learn that their voices count—that they can act effectively on their values in the larger world.

Frances Moore Lappé is the author or coauthor of 17 books, including Hope's Edge (2002), Democracy's Edge (2005), and Getting a Grip 2: Clarity, Creativity and Courage for the World We Really Want (2010). She is a founder and principal of the Small Planet Institute in Cambridge, Massachusetts (www.smallplanet.org).

Coventry, Rhode Island students present their anti-vandalism project to their State's Attorney General.

Student Ownership

Students are the driving force in planning and implementing service-learning, gaining greater confidence and heightened enthusiasm for learning as they help define problems and implement solutions. In KIDS service-learning projects, students assess needs through a Guided Discovery process facilitated by their teacher (who ensures academic integrity by helping students identify community needs that align with the curriculum). Both teachers and community members work alongside students and share in learning, acting more as partners than experts.

Through a facilitated process of investigation and research, students take ownership of both the problem and the solution. They routinely make decisions in small group work, classroom meetings, and planning with community members. Service-learning projects often generate enthusiasm and a sense of adventure among students, which may translate at first into commotion and confusion (with simultaneous committee discussions, maps and diagrams spread about, and overflowing flip charts), but ultimately results in authentic student learning.

Young people are not only our future, they are our present. Through the KIDS service-learning process, students acquire a voice and find they have the power to make a difference. Often, students with different talents emerge as leaders through the problem-solving process, becoming essential resources as they address current issues. Participants learn about their strengths, and may demonstrate unprecedented creativity and responsibility (see sidebar on resiliency).

Key Elements of Student Ownership

▶ **Student-driven:** students select, plan and implement projects

▶ **Adventure:** projects involve challenge and risk-taking

▶ **Partnerships:** students and adults are equal partners

▶ **Self-awareness:** students explore their strengths to set goals and solve problems

▶ **Students Matter:** students learn that they have the power to make a difference

The term "student ownership" implies that students make meaningful decisions throughout the process, but it does not mean that students always identify problems/needs and plans on their own. Teachers play a critical role in selecting and implementing projects, listening to and guiding students toward community needs and problems that fit well with the curriculum and other school dynamics (such as time constraints). The next two chapters offer detailed guidance on how to facilitate students' exploration of potential topics, helping ensure that their projects incorporate both student ownership and academic integrity.

Fostering Resilience by Bonnie Benard

Resiliency refers to the innate, self-righting capacity present in all human beings that enables them to grow and develop, even in the presence of serious risk factors like growing up in violent or abusive families or living in poverty-stricken communities.

Long-term studies of children facing these adversities have consistently found that at least 50 percent (and usually closer to two-thirds) of these youth grow up to be socially competent, caring adults who have a sense of identity, self-awareness, purpose and hope. A constellation of three interrelated protective factors appear consistently in the family, school or community life of youth who overcome the odds:

▶ caring relationships;

▶ positive and high expectations; and

▶ opportunities for meaningful participation and contribution.

KIDS Consortium provides an inspiring model of service-learning that succeeds, ultimately, because the adults are not trying to "fix" kids, but rather are coming from a belief system that views youth as having within them everything they need to be successful. The young people, in turn, manifest all the predicted attributes: social competence, a sense of identity and personal boundaries, motivation, persistence, optimism and, most importantly, spiritual connectedness and a sense of meaning.

Bonnie Benard has more than 25 years of experience helping children and youth live healthier, drug-free lives. She is the author of Resiliency: What We Have Learned (2004) and Fostering Resiliency in Kids: Protective Factors in the Family, School and Community (1991).

"Our students worked with KIDS Consortium on several projects, and every experience has been transformational! Because we are a school for extremely disaffected and at-risk young people, it's a particular challenge to help them find relevance in academic work. When we agreed to enlist our students as planners of the KIDS 2008 Student Summit, we really could never have imagined what was in store for our students! Staff members from KIDS Consortium were nothing short of heroic in their support, treating our students with dignity and respect as they muddled through the early stages of planning. They kept the integrity of student voice and choice sacred, even through rough beginnings, changing ideas, and various disappointments. Then, little by little, an amazing plan emerged! The culminating event was a spectacular success, a defining moment for kids who had experienced lifetimes of marginalization, failure, isolation, and fear, but now stood on stage—guiding an audience of 300 people through a two-day extravaganza of service-learning, team-building, and entertainment."

— *Pender Makin, director of The REAL School, Southern Maine*

The Benefits of Service-Learning

Service-learning can provide numerous benefits to all those who participate, with positive impacts that ripple outward. Enhancing the skills and efficacy of individual students, service-learning helps them succeed in school and in life. Moreover, service-learning fosters connections and collaboration, strengthening the culture of schools and the fabric of the larger community. The positive effects of service-learning occur on many levels simultaneously and often extend well beyond the span of a single project.

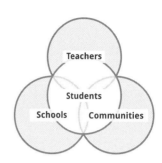

How the KIDS Model Benefits *Students*

In two studies* of KIDS Consortium programs conducted between 2004 and 2009 that involved more than 1,500 middle and high school students across New England, service-learning participants were almost 1.5 times more likely than comparison students to show an increase in:

▶ civic efficacy (their sense of being able to make a difference);

▶ interest in future involvement in civic affairs; and

▶ volunteering.

Service-learning students were also significantly more likely than comparison students to report gains on measures of civic skills, such as the ability to:

▶ identify important community problems/needs;

▶ use multiple sources to research a community problem;

▶ compare pros and cons of different solutions to a problem;

▶ communicate ideas to others; and

▶ work effectively on a team.

On average, service-learning students were 1.75 times more likely to report an increase on an overall measure of civic skills; and they were more than twice as likely to show a gain than the comparison students, and more likely to show greater gains.

Impact of KIDS Consortium Support on the Civic, Academic and Social Outcomes Among Student Survey Respondents: Three Years of New England Learn and Serve America, Key Findings, May 2011, Center for Youth and Communities, Heller School of Social Policy and Management, Brandeis University; KIDSCAN and Living Democracy Evaluation, Key Findings, February 2007, Center for Youth and Communities, Heller School of Social Policy and Management, Brandeis University.

"Closing the achievement gap requires that we ensure students have the necessary academic skills in reading and math; but it also requires that we provide them with a sense of empowerment through classroom culture, inquiry-oriented curricula, and service-learning opportunities... The awakening of students' awareness of, and belief in, their own inner strength and their capability to effect meaningful change transforms self-defeating attitudes into a positive perception of themselves as individuals who can take control of their own lives, and make a contribution to the life of their community, through the knowledge and skills they gain in their school experience."

— Sheldon Berman, superintendent and service-learning advocate

How the KIDS Model Benefits *Teachers and Schools*

Service-learning projects can improve the capacity of schools and school systems to:

▶ foster more caring classrooms and schools;

▶ offer opportunities for differentiated instruction and learning (meeting various needs and learning styles of students);

▶ reenergize teachers by allowing them to connect their ideals and values with their educational practice;

▶ promote collaboration among teachers;

▶ adopt new teaching structures and schedules;

▶ provide fulfilling ways for parents and community members to work with youth as experts and mentors;

▶ foster modes of teaching that incorporate key school reform ideas (such as hands-on, experiential and authentic learning); and

▶ provide opportunities for teachers to use alternative methods of student assessment.

When surveyed by KIDS Consortium and Brandeis University, more than 900 teachers who used the KIDS service-learning model with their students reported marked improvements in students' motivation, collaboration and problem-solving skills, alongside their own increased satisfaction (averaged over a 9-year period from 2001-2009):

▶ 90 percent reported that KIDS projects increased student engagement in learning (2006-2009 data);

▶ 94 percent reported that KIDS projects made teaching more rewarding;

▶ 96 percent reported that KIDS projects helped students learn to work with others;

▶ 91 percent reported that KIDS projects helped students become better problem-solvers; and

▶ 94 percent reported that KIDS projects helped students develop leadership skills (2006-2009 data).

How the KIDS Model Benefits *Communities*

KIDS service-learning projects offer communities a way to:

▶ raise awareness of community needs and undertake beneficial projects (that local organizations might not otherwise have resources to work on);

▶ forge creative partnerships between school and community members, increasing understanding of each other;

▶ engage young people in the process of solving community problems;

▶ provide opportunities for community organizations and issues to gain positive media coverage; and

▶ increase citizen participation now and in the future by cultivating the next generation of community leaders.

Survey results, gathered from more than 350 community organizations that have worked on KIDS service-learning projects with K-12 students (compiled by KIDS Consortium and Brandeis University and averaged over nine years from 2001-2009), indicate how successful this approach is at improving relationships and meeting real community needs:

▶ 95 percent reported that student projects met real community needs;

▶ 91 percent reported that service-learning experiences improved community attitudes toward youth; and

▶ 88 percent reported that service-learning improved school-community relations.

Moreover, nearly all respondents (96 percent) indicated that they will continue to work with students on service-learning projects in the future.

The Framework for KIDS Service-Learning Projects

Research and evaluations of service-learning over the past two decades clearly indicate that the quality of implementation impacts the outcomes for both student learning and service in the community. Our own experiences working with teachers and students have helped us gain a practical understanding of the kinds of tools and structures that help adults and students implement quality service-learning projects.

Using knowledge from the service-learning field about quality practice and our own evaluations and experiences, we created the following Framework for KIDS Service-Learning. The Framework presents a "recipe" for translating the three KIDS principles from a set of concepts into an implementation process. We encourage you to think about the Framework as a guide, not a rigid prescription. The elements of the Framework are all important for quality practice, but the time you decide to spend on each one and the order in which you implement various elements will depend on many factors.

"Service-learning has strengthened our organizations by providing a link between education, civic involvement and real-life experiences."

— *Jan Barton, Barnstable Town Council, Barnstable, Massachusetts*

KIDS Framework

The following figure depicts the steps that KIDS service-learning projects typically involve.

1. define service-learning;
2. discover needs and problems;
3. investigate problems;
4. research solutions;
5. decide on a project;
6. plan the project;
7. implement the plan; and
8. evaluate impacts.

Following these steps can help ensure that your project is well-planned and carefully executed. All of the steps should be completed, but their scope and sequence may vary depending on the nature of the project.

As you follow these steps, do not lose sight of the Framework's "clouds:"

▶ collaborative environment;
▶ reflection;
▶ public relations;
▶ celebration; and
▶ curriculum, instruction and assessment.

These concepts are essential elements of all KIDS service-learning projects that happen on an ongoing basis throughout the process, and can be adapted to meet the needs of individual projects. Pay continual attention to them as you follow the Framework steps. A blank framework planning sheet can be found in the Appendix on page 95.

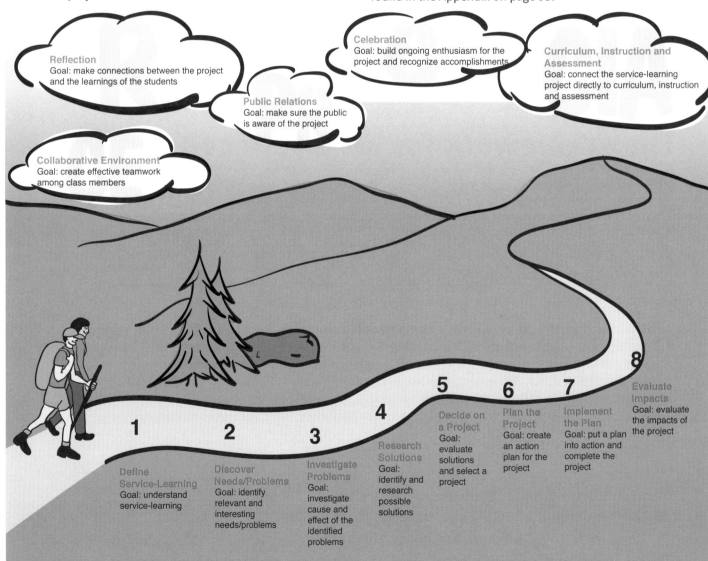

Reflection
Goal: make connections between the project and the learnings of the students

Celebration
Goal: build ongoing enthusiasm for the project and recognize accomplishments

Curriculum, Instruction and Assessment
Goal: connect the service-learning project directly to curriculum, instruction and assessment

Public Relations
Goal: make sure the public is aware of the project

Collaborative Environment
Goal: create effective teamwork among class members

1 Define Service-Learning
Goal: understand service-learning

2 Discover Needs/Problems
Goal: identify relevant and interesting needs/problems

3 Investigate Problems
Goal: investigate cause and effect of the identified problems

4 Research Solutions
Goal: identify and research possible solutions

5 Decide on a Project
Goal: evaluate solutions and select a project

6 Plan the Project
Goal: create an action plan for the project

7 Implement the Plan
Goal: put a plan into action and complete the project

8 Evaluate Impacts
Goal: evaluate the impacts of the project

As the field of service-learning has grown nationally, so has the commitment to ensuring the highest quality service-learning. In 2008, the service-learning field released new national standards to enhance the practice of service-learning in diverse educational settings across the nation. The KIDS service-learning model, through its three core principles and framework, helps educators incorporate national standards (see below) through a step-by-step process that has been tested and refined over two decades. For a detailed overview of the national K-12 Service-Learning Standards for Quality Practice, visit the National Youth Leadership Council website at www.nylc.org/standards.

KIDS projects commonly involve all class members, but the model can be readily adapted for use by individuals or small groups of students. In some cases, the class may want to divide up into teams and pursue several related projects. The framework outlined on the previous page applies to all KIDS projects, whether they are completed by a single student, a team of students, an entire class, or multiple classes (see page 21).

How the KIDS Framework Helps Meet K-12 National Service-Learning Standards

Where the KIDS Framework helps to meet standards	K-12 National Standards
STUDENTS: ▶ work w/ community partners throughout the framework ▶ discover relevant and interesting needs/problems ▶ investigate the cause and effect of problems on all stakeholders ▶ research multiple solutions before deciding on best option ▶ plan and implement a solution ▶ develop effective teamwork and collaboration skills to foster mutual respect and multiple perspectives	YOUTH VOICE PARTNERSHIPS MEANINGFUL SERVICE DIVERSITY
STUDENTS: ▶ demonstrate curriculum objectives and engage in direct and independent instruction and multiple forms of assessment ▶ engage in multiple reflection activities to connect project experiences and learning (affective and cognitive) ▶ communicate the project's progress to others to build public relations ▶ celebrate to build ongoing enthusiasm for the project and recognize accomplishments ▶ evaluate the impacts of the project on the specified problem/need	LINKS TO CURRICULUM PROGRESS MONITORING REFLECTION
Meeting the goals of each of the framework steps will ensure that community and student outcomes are met. Sufficient time must be devoted to implementing the steps of the framework for the integrity of the process to be upheld.	DURATION & INTENSITY

www.nylc.org/standards

How to Use This Guide

This book guides you through the KIDS Framework, helping you plan and facilitate a successful service-learning process. The information and tools included are for use at elementary, middle and high school levels. While you may choose to focus on those chapters most relevant to your situation, we recommend that you read Chapters 2 and 3—at a minimum—as they provide essential background for subsequent activities and tools.

▶ **Chapter 2** suggests *planning to do before introducing service-learning to students* (the Curriculum, Instruction and Assessment "cloud").

▶ **Chapter 3** outlines ways to *engage students in the initial phase of service-learning* (Step 1 of the KIDS Framework, and the Collaborative Environment and Reflection "clouds").

▶ **Chapter 4** covers the steps involved in *discovering and investigating problems* (Steps 2-3 of the Framework).

▶ **Chapter 5** guides the *selection of appropriate solutions* (Steps 4-5 of the Framework and the Public Relations and Celebration "clouds").

▶ **Chapter 6** describes how to *plan, implement and evaluate a solution* (Steps 6-8 of the Framework).

▶ **Chapter 7** recommends ways to *make service-learning part of your future teaching practice and environment.*

Throughout the guide, there are numerous tools to help you plan and carry out your project. Many of these interactive exercises engage students, encouraging their ownership of the project. Clean copies of tool worksheets are available in the Appendix to photocopy for classroom use. You may find these tools helpful for activities beyond your service-learning project; we encourage you to adapt them as needed.

Sidebars throughout the book entitled "Election Project" help illustrate how steps of the KIDS Framework play out in practice through a service-learning project designed to increase voter turnout.

"The national quality standards for service-learning have significantly helped with our training of teachers, administrators and community partners. Using those standards in conjunction with the KIDS Framework has generated a much deeper and more engaged understanding of both the what (national standards) and the how (KIDS Framework) of service-learning. It's critical to understand the relationship between the two."

— *Matt McLane, Service-Learning Coordinator, Montpelier, VT Public Schools*

Chapter 2:
Plan and Prepare

Case Study: Promoting Literacy Among Afghan Girls and Women

Before entering the sixth grade, students at the Pierce School in Brookline, Massachusetts read Deborah Ellis' novel *The Breadwinner* about the oppressed life of an Afghan girl. After discussing this book and related articles, the sixth-graders heard a young Afghan woman speak about her childhood experiences living in Kabul under the Taliban.

Staff from a local nonprofit, Barakat, Inc., helped students learn about the identity, education and opportunity of Afghan girls (including the startling fact that nearly 57 percent of Afghan males are literate but only 13 percent of Afghan women and girls can read and write). After conducting further research, students decided to help Barakat with education, outreach and fundraising. Their service-learning project complemented the district's grade 6 social studies curriculum, which involves the study of Islam.

Staff of Barakat maintained close communications through letters, e-mail and return visits as each student committee met several times each week and formed subcommittees as needed. "These subcommittees did impressive independent work," teacher Melissa London reflects. "Once their initial tasks were completed, they often devised additional tasks for themselves!" Education Committee members got feedback from classroom teachers on three lesson plans they developed (one aimed at K-2 students; a second at 3rd-4th graders and a third at 5th-8th graders).

Fundraising Committee members planned events to generate both attention and money: raffles, bake sales, garage sales, a school-wide envelope drive and a customized fundraising website (using FirstGiving). To encourage participation in Barakat's Walk for Literacy fundraiser, students posted a "Wall of Walkers" at the school announcing how many people had registered.

Outreach Committee members worked with the school's technology specialist to create a blog, "PHAR: Pierce Helps Afghanistan Read," and wrote letters for the school newsletter and local newspaper. Students from all three committees used the group blog to share observations and celebrate their achievements. "There were enough genuine moments of positive press or feedback along the way that students never lost interest or momentum," observes London. "The enthusiasm was organic and largely self-generated and self-sustaining."

Partners at Barakat shared their feedback in appreciative letters to students, writing in one: "It was pretty amazing what you've been able to accomplish in such a short amount of time. Everything that you've accomplished in your school speaks to the power of working together as a part of a team."

The impact of students' efforts was clear at the Walk for Literacy event in October 2009, where 40 percent of participants came from the Pierce School community. Barakat publicly acknowledged the students for raising $8,000—helping fund a year of schooling for more than 200 Afghan girls. Students later reflected on their learning by completing a project summary and a longer narrative.

How Do I Begin?

When first introduced to the KIDS principles outlined in Chapter One, many teachers ask how they can balance curriculum requirements (academic integrity) with their desire to meaningfully empower students (student ownership). You may share this question, or feel constrained in your classroom planning by the expansion of state and local requirements and the growing focus on measurable learning outcomes. Service-learning projects can help meet these demands in creative and integrative ways that renew your enthusiasm for teaching and engage students in meaningful learning. Balancing academic integrity and student ownership takes careful planning, with some of it happening before you introduce service-learning to your students (the subject of Chapter 3). This chapter will help you make preliminary decisions about project parameters and lay the groundwork for a successful service-learning experience that fully engages students and ensures they fulfill curricular demands.

As you begin contemplating your service-learning project, it may be helpful to read about some model service-learning projects. For lists of project ideas related to various content areas, see page 96 in the Appendix and the "Our Model" section of the KIDS website at www.kidsconsortium.org.

Entry Point Options

By understanding your situation and how much flexibility it affords, you can select the most appropriate entry point for your service-learning project. This context will be important to consider as you introduce service-learning to your students and frame a process for identifying how best to start your project. Consider such factors as:

▶ Curriculum requirements (e.g., What are your grade level expectations? Curricular objectives and outcomes? Units of study?);

▶ School/classroom structure (e.g., Are you in a fully contained elementary classroom? Are you team-teaching? Are you part of a content area department? Are you a specialist?);

▶ Class size and schedule (e.g., What is your class size? How long are class periods? Do you have options to meet with students for longer periods of time?); and

▶ Student and/or community interest (e.g., Are there problems or needs that have been identified?).

Balancing Student Ownership and Academic Integrity

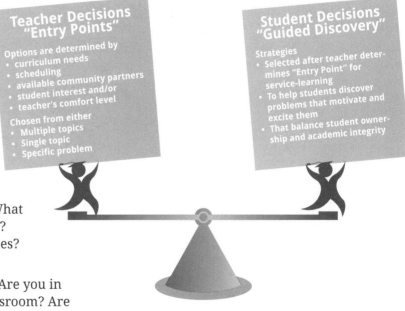

Teacher Decisions "Entry Points"

Options are determined by
- curriculum needs
- scheduling
- available community partners
- student interest and/or
- teacher's comfort level

Chosen from either
- Multiple topics
- Single topic
- Specific problem

Student Decisions "Guided Discovery"

Strategies
- Selected after teacher determines "Entry Point" for service-learning
- To help students discover problems that motivate and excite them
- That balance student ownership and academic integrity

ENTRY POINTS

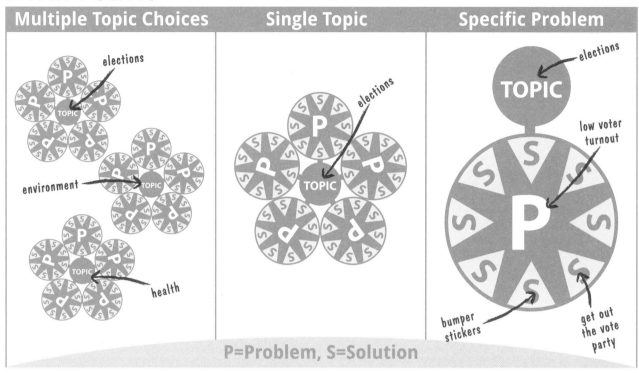

| Multiple Topic Choices | Single Topic | Specific Problem |

P=Problem, S=Solution

You can choose one of three entry points for embarking on a service-learning project, ranging from a broad multiple topic approach (if you have considerable curricular flexibility) to a single topic approach (somewhat more focused but still affording students latitude to select a specific problem or need) to a Specific Problem (the most focused option, and a good choice if you have limited time).

▶ **Multiple Topic Choices:** Encourage students to freely select and explore multiple topics of interest in order to discover a service-learning problem or need. For example, students could brainstorm a list of multiple topics of interest (environment, health, hunger, elections). They might then do local tours and invite speakers to their class to help them learn more. After generating a list of problems/needs that interest them, the class could focus on a single problem or divide into teams to address multiple problems.

▶ **Single Topic:** Focus students on one topic which they explore in order to discover a service-learning problem or need. If a class focused on elections, for example, they could visit City Hall to meet with the elections clerk and learn more about past election concerns and upcoming elections. Students could then generate a list of related problems and either settle on one or divide into teams to address multiple problems.

▶ **Specific Problem:** Focus students on a specific problem or need that they decide to address. For example, a local elections clerk contacts a social studies teacher to ask for help with the problem of low voter turnout. The teacher shares this information with students and the students decide to interview the clerk to learn more about the problem and how they might help increase voter turnout. Students then choose to address this problem.

Once you've determined the most appropriate entry point for a service-learning project, you'll be ready to undertake Guided Discovery with your students. It's important to select Guided Discovery activities appropriate to your entry point. Poor matches (e.g., a specific problem entry point paired with far-reaching guided discovery activities) can frustrate both you and your students. Chapter 4 covers Guided Discovery in more detail, but it's helpful to introduce the process here as you consider your project entry point.

How to Handle Large Groups

Teachers responsible for multiple sections of larger courses may assume that service-learning isn't practical with big student groups. It is a viable option still: you just need to introduce service-learning in stages. Here are some ideas to consider:

▶ **Start Small—with One Class or Section:** Try piloting a service-learning experience initially with just one class or section to gain experience and confidence in your ability to facilitate the KIDS process. Begin with a single topic or specific problem as your entry point.

▶ **Multiple Sections, One at a Time:** Consider facilitating multiple service-learning projects throughout the year (e.g., Section One engages in service-learning as part of a fall trimester unit; Section Two in the winter trimester; and Section Three in the spring trimester).

▶ **Multiple Sections at the Same Time:** If you choose to engage more than one section or class in service-learning at a time, you can consider several options. With each group of students, you'll want to decide whether to use similar or different entry points and approaches (see page 61 — Approaches in Chapter 5). Some options include:

- All sections work on the same topic, but each section finds a different problem(s) to tackle;
- All sections work on the same problem, but each section finds a different solution(s) or approach(es) to solving the problem: or
- All sections work on the same problem and the same solution, but each section breaks into teams to take on different roles and responsibilities as they plan and implement the solution.

When multiple classes work on the same topic and/or problem, begin by having each class participate in the first four steps of the KIDS Framework: define service-learning, discover needs/problems, investigate problems, and research solutions. Then, as a means to facilitate communication among classes throughout the project, have students consider:

▶ Creating a project web page (e.g., Wiki or Facebook);

▶ Using a project management tool (such as Basecamp or Groupsite) to post updates and next steps; and

▶ Electing a representative or two from each class to serve on an Advisory Board (meeting at lunch or after school) that communicates and reports back on progress and challenges.

Be sure to provide structured planning time for students to work on their service-learning plans, helping to establish consistency and further develop the collaborative environment. For example, designate particular days and/or times for students in all sections to share updates, reflect, make decisions, etc.

Students from one class collected and analyzed data about ways to "green" their school from other students in the school.

Guided Discovery

Guided Discovery is a facilitated process of inquiry through which the teacher guides students to discover community topics, problems and needs associated with the curriculum they may want to address. The initial focus is on learning about concerns, not on defining a specific solution. Through the discovery process, students become engaged and begin caring about the issues. Rather than being instructed to "do this" by a teacher or administrator, they are asking, "can we positively address this problem or need?"

Guided Discovery builds youth voice—the input young people provide in developing and implementing projects, plans, and policies to guide service-learning efforts. Initially, students may know little about needs or problems in their community so teachers need to create experiences that foster first-hand understanding through such means as field trips, guest speakers, literature circles and review of available data. Through these experiences, students become motivated to seek solutions and make a difference. Numerous studies tracking service-learning outcomes (e.g., K-12 Service-Learning Standards for Quality Practice: An Annotated Bibiography, RMC Research Corporation and National Youth Leadership Council, 2008)) attest to how student voice fosters greater self-confidence and personal efficacy among students, as well as better interpersonal communication, critical thinking skills, academic engagement and civic participation.

Community and business partners in Lisbon, CT present their problems and needs to teachers and students at a community partner fair.

Tool: Shift from Solution to Community Need

Building student ownership is vital to the success of service-learning. Remember your role is to facilitate students discovering topics/needs/problems; resist the temptation to provide a solution/project. The first example below demonstrates how a teacher can shift from offering a solution/project to introducing community needs/problems. Complete the remaining examples to gain practice shifting from solution/ project to needs/problems. Use the right column to brainstorm specific ways to guide students in their discovery of the identified needs/problems.

"I have a really good project for my class...The town owns a huge parcel of land behind the school building. It would be perfect for my students to work on a trail project..."	
Possible Community Needs/Problems:	**How Can Students Discover the Need/Problem?**
• *Walking access to school from local neighborhoods*	• *Invite local pathways committee to discuss ways to encourage more walking/biking to school*
• *Lack of public open spaces or hiking opportunities*	• *Invite local Conservation Commission or hiking club to discuss existing trails and need for expanded opportunities*
• *Childhood obesity and community need for healthy exercise*	• *Invite school nurse to discuss obesity (physical problems, causes, and societal costs)*

I am going to have my students interview veterans and write oral histories.	
Possible Community Needs/Problems:	**How Can Students Discover the Need/Problem?**

In the unit we're doing on plants, I think my students should create a garden in front of the school.	
Possible Community Needs/Problems:	**How Can Students Discover the Need/Problem?**

I was thinking that during our Energy unit, I'd have students work to get solar panels for the school.	
Possible Community Needs/Problems:	**How Can Students Discover the Need/Problem?**

Connect to the Community

As you begin working with students to identify needs and problems, help them consider the full breadth and diversity of their community, such as school staff (including often overlooked members like bus drivers, cafeteria staff, and custodians), local residents, professionals and organizations with related expertise, and potential partners and funders. Partners from different facets of the community can bring first-hand knowledge of community concerns, as well as valuable expertise and infectious enthusiasm to help energize and inform the students' research. Think about ways to incorporate multiple perspectives, engaging the opinions and concerns of varied stakeholders.

Community partners can play a wide range of roles in service-learning, such as providing funding or resources for a project; serving as an expert; or being a truly reciprocal partner, where students work in concert with the community organization and it benefits directly from the students' efforts. Clarify early on with each partner organization the extent of its commitment. Arrange a meeting to discuss your educational goals for the project, what students hope to contribute, and what role the partner might play (see Tool: What to Discuss in Early Conversations). Invite community partners to share their concerns and negotiate a mutually beneficial relationship. It can be helpful to strategize with community partners about potential allies who might provide in-kind or financial support for your project. Consider outlining roles and responsibilities in a letter or agreement document. On the next page is a sample letter from a teacher to a community partner as part of the Election Project that was used to ensure that both parties have a clear understanding of their responsibilities.

Throughout the process, remind students to express their appreciation for the support of community partners, through letters, public recognition and other creative means.

Tool: What to Discuss in Early Conversations

Project Goals: What are the goals/objectives for the teacher? For the community partner? For the students?

Methods of Communication: Exchange contact information and determine when/how is the best time to connect. Some teachers prefer e-mail while others prefer phone calls before or after school.

Project Scope: How much time is required? When will specific dates and times be established?

Fundraising: How will this project be funded? Who will help raise funds and how?

Training: Is extra time needed to train teachers or students? What does this training involve?

Other Topics

Safety and Paperwork: Review school policies regarding student confidentiality (e.g., taking and using photographs, and obtaining permission forms). Who will collect and have on file the necessary permission slips and emergency contact information? Who will provide first aid kits and other safety equipment?

Transportation: Is outside transportation (involving buses, carpools and/or parent volunteers) necessary? If so, who will arrange it?

Equipment/Supplies: What equipment or supplies are needed and who will provide these? Is any special training needed to use the equipment?

Student Supervision and Discipline: Will other adults/volunteers be needed for supervision (e.g., on field trips)? How will inappropriate behavior be handled?

Media Contact: Will project participants contact newspapers/television? Will students draft a press release? What review process will there be for media outreach materials?

Project Documentation: Does this project need to be documented? Who will do this and how will it happen?

[Adapted with permission from the Mount Desert Island Water Quality Coalition]

Election Project: Writing the Community Partner

Dear Ms. Hernandez (Town Clerk),

Thank you for meeting with me last week and for your willingness to participate in a service-learning project with my social studies class. The students have been engaging in lively discussions about the upcoming election and look forward to learning more about the voting process when they visit the Town Hall in early September. Using the information they collect from you, students will be able to narrow the focus of their project to a particular problem and begin researching possible solutions.

What follows is an outline of the project, including the roles that we discussed last week. I am excited about working with you as a valued community partner during our service-learning experience this semester.

Project Overview
Students investigate problems around the topic of elections and the voting process. After further research and investigation, students will implement a particular solution to be completed on or before Election Day. They will spend time working with you, evaluating their community impact within a few weeks after the Election. By doing this project, students will gain better understanding of the differences between the major political parties; the electoral process and needs related to it, and their own political beliefs. They will use collaborative planning and problem- solving with peers and adults to make a difference in their community.

Timeline
Students will begin planning in early September (including a field trip to meet with you at the Town Hall) and the entire service-learning project will be completed (including evaluating impacts) by Thanksgiving. Weekly classroom planning meetings will be held to update/celebrate progress and troubleshoot. Thank you for agreeing to attend at least three of these meetings (one per month).

Teacher/Community Partner Expectations

The TEACHER agrees to:

▶ Set dates for project events (finalize and communicate by September 1)

▶ Instruct students how to create a timeline and provide timeline for partner agreement

▶ Attend trainings provided by the community partner and organize follow-up activities for students

▶ Arrange and pay for bussing to the Town Hall

▶ Instruct students on needed project planning

▶ Provide community partner with student names

▶ Make sure students have appropriate safety release forms signed (e.g., field trips, photos release, etc.)

▶ Assess student learning from the project

▶ Find additional school and community volunteers needed to complete the work projects outlined

▶ Work with students to document project

The TOWN CLERK agrees to:

▶ Offer an orientation/training to students and teachers about the selected election issues (September field trip to Town Hall)

▶ Host at least one field trip in which students conduct on-site research and planning work (rescheduling as needed to accommodate weather cancellations)

▶ Provide project-related support to teachers and students through emails, phone calls, and periodic visits (attending at least three planning meetings with students)

▶ Ensure a safe environment for student visits

▶ Help students evaluate the impact of their project

▶ Work with the students as colleagues, simultaneously respecting and building their capacities

Please e-mail me and let me know if this represents everything we discussed at our meeting last week. Thanks again for your interest in this service-learning project.

Sincerely,

Andrea Smith (Teacher)

"Do our classrooms provide students with a sense of community in which they have voice, experience connection to others, and understand their impact on others and the classroom as a whole? Does our curriculum engage students in questioning and exploration so they develop a sense of mastery in thinking through problems and producing high-quality work? Does our instruction provide opportunities for students to apply their knowledge and skills for the benefit of others and the community?"

— *Sheldon Berman, Superintendent, Louisville, Kentucky, and service-learning advocate*

Curriculum, Instruction and Assessment

Teachers need to shape service-learning so it fits within existing curriculum objectives and is not an add-on. A facilitated process of Guided Discovery (see earlier Entry Points Options on page 19) can help balance student ownership with the demands of local and state curriculum. Whether you begin by identifying curriculum units or community problems, both need to correlate.

While students design many aspects of their service-learning projects, teachers need to sketch out the contours of the process so they know how to introduce it. Before embarking on Guided Discovery work with your students, consider completing the Project Overview Circle (a blank form is in the Appendix on page 97). This exercise helps determine your project parameters—starting with your entry point and moving around the circle to potential community partners, level of student ownership, and curriculum links. The following example, from the election project, demonstrates how this exercise can help lay the groundwork for appropriate assessments.

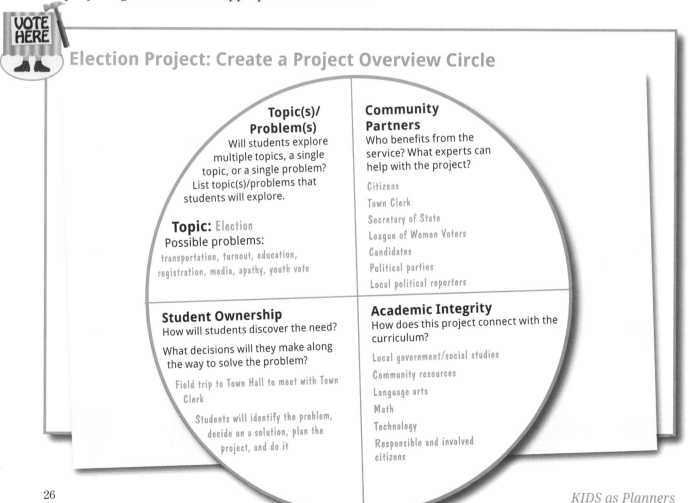

Election Project: Create a Project Overview Circle

Topic(s)/Problem(s)
Will students explore multiple topics, a single topic, or a single problem? List topic(s)/problems that students will explore.

Topic: Election
Possible problems:
transportation, turnout, education, registration, media, apathy, youth vote

Community Partners
Who benefits from the service? What experts can help with the project?

Citizens
Town Clerk
Secretary of State
League of Women Voters
Candidates
Political parties
Local political reporters

Student Ownership
How will students discover the need?

What decisions will they make along the way to solve the problem?

Field trip to Town Hall to meet with Town Clerk

Students will identify the problem, decide on a solution, plan the project, and do it

Academic Integrity
How does this project connect with the curriculum?

Local government/social studies
Community resources
Language arts
Math
Technology
Responsible and involved citizens

Weave Together Learning

To help link the service-learning process to your curricular objectives, you may want to map (or web) what students need to do or learn. The web may be interdisciplinary, as in the following election project example (a blank form for this tool appears in the Appendix on page 98), or specific to a single content area—depending on your teaching situation. If you teach social studies, for example, your web might include content and skills under history, economics, civics and geography. Note that five items in the web are circled as ideas for potential assessment. The one highlighted item appears in the Planning Backwards example on page 33, demonstrating how curriculum, instruction and assessment are aligned in the election project.

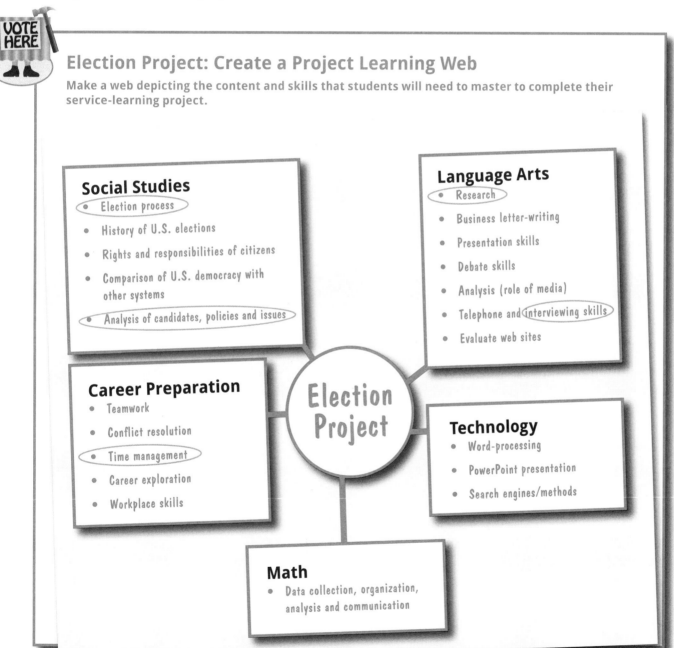

Election Project: Create a Project Learning Web

Make a web depicting the content and skills that students will need to master to complete their service-learning project.

Social Studies
- Election process
- History of U.S. elections
- Rights and responsibilities of citizens
- Comparison of U.S. democracy with other systems
- Analysis of candidates, policies and issues

Language Arts
- Research
- Business letter-writing
- Presentation skills
- Debate skills
- Analysis (role of media)
- Telephone and interviewing skills
- Evaluate web sites

Career Preparation
- Teamwork
- Conflict resolution
- Time management
- Career exploration
- Workplace skills

Election Project

Technology
- Word-processing
- PowerPoint presentation
- Search engines/methods

Math
- Data collection, organization, analysis and communication

Means of Assessment

It's helpful at this early juncture to consider the service-learning process in terms of two sets of outcomes: student learning and community impact. As you explore possible topics, consider both of these measures, as they will be key means of assessment during your project and upon its completion.

Service-Learning Benefits the Community and Benefits the Participants

**SERVICE
Impacts Community**

**LEARNING
Impacts Students**

Assessments allow students to demonstrate their command of knowledge or skills through an authentic task, while helping teachers identify whether further instruction on content or skills is required. Assessments can also be products or performances that reflect the overall learning experience (encompassing many learning outcomes), and allow students to demonstrate their mastery of relevant learning standards, and contribution to the community (e.g., formal presentations to a town council or school board, exhibitions or portfolios).

As you plan your project, consider ways to incorporate different kinds of assessments during and after the project. For example, fifth graders at the Martel School in Lewiston, Maine undertook a community gardening project involving two assessments tasks (each student completed an independent soil analysis and wrote portions of a story for local newspapers explaining the importance of community gardens). At the end of the year, all students made formal presentations to fourth-grade classes to build their interest in sustaining the garden.

In the election project example, assessments of student work included letters to the editor, press releases, journal entries, and quizzes, as well as oral presentations made to the Town Council, local elections clerk, and League of Women Voters. You may wish to consider incorporating some of the following means of assessment as you plan your project:

▶ Reports that include research methodology, findings and recommendations

▶ Oral presentations or demonstrations to peers, school board or local government

▶ Public performances (e.g., a play, forum, public service announcement, teaching or television interview)

▶ Field notes and observations

▶ Letters and press releases

▶ Learning logs or book response journals in which students share ideas and questions prompted by lessons and reading assignments

▶ Portfolio of student products (including writing, audio or video productions, and maps)

▶ Products of community value (e.g., a sign, mural, museum exhibit or brochure)

- ▶ One-on-one conferences
- ▶ Self and peer assessments
- ▶ Communications products (e.g., a poster, logo, multimedia presentation or web page)
- ▶ Documents that conform to professional standards (e.g., a scale model, master plan or grant proposal)
- ▶ Procedures that meet technical standards (e.g., water-quality monitoring or cataloging artifacts)
- ▶ Standards-based lesson plans

Students and teachers assess their impact on the community problem/need by collecting data throughout the project and after their work is complete. For example, students may collect data on how many registered voters they spoke to, and what the actual local voter turnout was in the next local election.

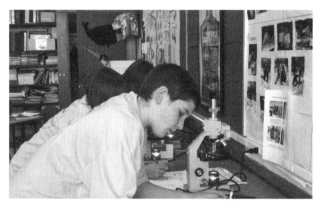

Consider ways to do assessments throughout the project, such as having students complete a water analysis as part of a habitat or watershed project.

Assess Progress with Rubrics

To ensure that assessments are closely aligned to curricular and learning objectives, you may want to consider creating rubrics—scoring tools that clearly document how well students are mastering given standards. Teachers and students can collaboratively create scoring tools that describe how students will demonstrate mastery of selected learning standards. These rubrics can be devised for many aspects of a project, from initial tasks like research or fieldwork to final activities like presentations. The sample rubric below was used in the election project to assess how students defended a position on a selected public policy issue.

Election Project: Rubric for Policy Position

Criteria/Content Standard & Performance Indicator	**1** Does Not Meet Standards	**2** Partially Meets Standard	**3** Meets Standard	**4** Exceeds Standard
Civics and Government A. Rights, Responsibilities & Participation 1. Develop and defend a position on a public policy issue within our democracy. A position on a public policy issue is given with or without arguments. If arguments are included, they are unclear and lack relevant facts, logic, and/ or details.	A position on a public policy issue is given and supported with fewer than three arguments, each adequately supported with relevant facts, logic and details.	A position on a public policy issue is given and supported with fewer than three arguments, each adequately supported with relevant facts, logic and details. A candidate's position on this policy is mentioned.	A position on a public policy issue is clearly developed and supported with at least three persuasive arguments. The arguments are developed using reliable and relevant facts, logic and details. There is a clear comparison to a candidate's position on this policy.	A position on a public policy issue is thoroughly developed and supported with at least three highly persuasive arguments. Each argument is richly developed using facts, logic, supporting examples, and details. There is a clear comparison to the position of multiple candidates.

Scoring tools can help students assess and reflect on their own performance and learning. To convey expectations for a project, distribute these tools, with clear criteria for quality work, to students as a task is assigned. At Edward Little High School in Auburn, Maine, students used the following Fieldwork Rubric to assess their daily performance and wrote journal entries reflecting on the tasks they undertook, the obstacles they encountered, and the accomplishments they achieved. Every few weeks, students met in conferences with teachers to discuss their journals and fieldwork.

At the end of their second semester, students prepared a portfolio using materials from their field work and classes (such as interviews, tests, essays, notes, research papers, sketches, labs and journals). They presented these in a structured, 45-minute exit performance to a panel of school and community members. Their exit performances proved to be a valuable means of demonstrating the knowledge and skills acquired through service-learning.

Tool: Fieldwork Rubric

	4	3	2	1	0
Time on task	90-100%	80-89%	70-79%	60-69%	Less than 60%
Positive impact	Makes strong positive impact	Makes positive impact	Makes moderate impact	Is indifferent	Makes negative impact
Self-discipline	Always demonstrates self-discipline	Consistently displays self-discipline	Generally displays self-discipline	Seldom displays self-discipline	Never displays self-discipline
Directions	Always listens to and understands directions	Consistently listens to and understands directions	Generally listens to and understands directions	Seldom listens to and understands directions	Never listens to and understands directions
Language	Always uses appropriate language	Consistently uses appropriate language	Occasionally uses inappropriate language by accident	Sometimes uses inappropriate language by habit	Deliberately uses inappropriate language
Tools & Equipment	Always takes responsibility for use and care of tools and equipment	Consistently takes responsibility for use and care of tools and equipment	Generally takes responsibility for use and care of tools and equipment	Seldom takes responsibility for use and care of tools and equipment	Never takes responsibility for use and care of tools and equipment

Tool: Oral Presentation Rubric

Category	Does Not Meet the Standards	Partially Meets the Standards	Meets the Standards	Exceeds the Standards
	F	D	C	B	A
Content	Demonstrates superficial or flawed knowledge of topic. No introduction is apparent. Main ideas are not clear.	Demonstrates inconsistent knowledge of topic. Introduction is vague. Few details support main ideas. Demonstrates little reflection on topic. Tie to service component is unclear.	Demonstrates consistent knowledge of topic. Introduction is clear. Main idea is clear. Details support main idea.Demonstrates some reflection on topic. Tie to service component is mentioned.	Demonstrates interest in and consistent knowledge of topic. Introduction is attention-getting. Main ideas are focused. Supporting details are varied and demonstrate logical conclusions. Clear evidence of reflection.	Demonstrates in-depth knowledge of topic. Introduction engages the audience. Main ideas are insightful. Supporting details are varied and demonstrate exemplary conclusions.Clear evidence of self-discovery and reflection.Tie to service component is clear.
Delivery	Demonstrates no reflection on topic. No mention of service component. Demonstrates no attention to audience. Speech is often difficult to understand. Gestures interfere with presentation.Clear that practice has not occurred. Reads from note cards or paper, does not look at audience. Pace interferes with presentation. Time requirements are not met.	Starts before audience is attending. Speech is difficult to understand at times. Gestures are minimal or stilted. Little evidence that practice has occurred. Glances at audience, refers to note cards frequently. Pace somewhat interferes with presentation. Time requirements are minimally met.	Gains the attention of the audience. Speech is clear most of the time. Gestures are controlled. Evident that practice has occurred. Looks around, refers to cards or paper. Pace is neither too fast or too slow. Time requirements are met.	Tie to service component is clear. Gains the nterest of the audience. Speech is clear. Gestures are utilized effectively. Presentation is polished.Makes eye contact, looks around, tells more than reads off cards or paper.Pace is neither too fast nor too slow. Time requirements are met.	Initial impact is strong. Speech is clear and animated. Gestures add significantly to the presentation. Student exudes self-confidence and is poised, has "stage presence." Eye contact is effective. Little reliance on script or cards. Presentation is sophisticated and passionate. Time requirements are met.
Question & Answer Period	Student does not answer questions or provides unrelated/flawed information. Response to questions demonstrates superficial or flawed knowledge of topic researched and/or project.	Student answers hesitantly and minimally. Response to questions demonstrates limited knowledge of the topic research and/or project.	Student answers questions with examples and detail. Responses to questions demonstrate adequate knowledge of the topic research and/or project.	Student answers questions fluently, confidently. Responses to questions demonstrate solid knowledge of the topic research and/or project.	Student answers questions with clear opinions. Confidently, and with evidence of self-reflection. Responses to questions demonstrate in-depth, cross-disciplinary knowledge of topic/project.
Visuals	Few required components of the visual are evident. Visual presentation is messy and organized. Graphs and charts contain errors or misrepresent information. Written parts contain many errors in grammar and mechanics. No mention of service component.	Most of the required components of the visual are evident. Presentation has some visual flaws and is somewhat unkempt. Charts and graphs have some errors. Written parts contain some errors in grammar and mechanics. Tie to service component is unclear.	All of the required components are evident. Presentation is neat and organized. Charts and graphs have few errors. Written parts have very few errors in grammar and mechanics. Tie to service component is mentioned.	All of the required components of the visual are evident. Presentation is visually attractive and neat. Charts and graphs are correct. Written parts have no errors in grammar and mechanics. Tie to service component is clear.	All required components of the visual are evident, additional parts enhance the visual. Presentation entices the viewer to look. Charts and graphs enhance the visual. Written parts contain no grammatical or mechanical errors. Presentation uses technology effectively. Tie to service component is clear.

Plan Backwards

"Planning backwards" is an approach for connecting curriculum, instruction and assessment that begins with identifying the learning objectives for student work. This model considers five important questions:

▶ What are the learning objectives? (i.e., your state/local standards)

▶ How will you assess prior student knowledge of these objectives?

▶ What instructional activities (e.g., mini-lessons, practice debates) will you use to teach objectives, including opportunities for students to practice their new knowledge and skills?

▶ What are the tasks (i.e., products and performances) by which students will demonstrate achievement of these objectives?

▶ What assessment tool (e.g., rubric, product descriptor) will you use to provide feedback to students?

The following chart illustrates the "planning backwards" process for one item (analysis of candidates, policies and issues) drawn from the election project web on page 27. A blank Planning Backwards chart can be found in the Appendix on page 99.

Reflection and Assessment in a Nutshell

Reflection:
To reflect—to bend back; to bend experiences back into your mind; to create a bridge between experience and learning.

Reflection—making connections and creating meaning by linking the experience and the students' learning.

Assessment:
To assess—from Latin assidere, to sit down beside

Assessment—feedback or evidence that demonstrates how students have met standards based on explicit criteria.

(Adapted from Rick Gordon and Linda Freese, Antioch University, New England)

Election Project: Planning Backwards – Curriculum, Instruction and Assessment

Learning Objective	Assessing Prior Knowledge	Instructional Activities	Assessment Tasks	Assessment Tool(s)
Social Studies Curriculum Standard: Civics A. Rights, Responsibilities, and Participation **Indicator:** HS 1: Develop and defend a position on a public policy issue within our democracy	Every student must fill in a KWL chart of what they know about public policy and candidate's positions, what they want to know, and how they might learn it.	Possible Instruction: ▶ Respect for diverse opinions in community and democracy ▶ Pertinent vocabulary ▶ What is public policy? ▶ Who are governing bodies? ▶ Candidate panel ▶ Interviewing skills ▶ Elements of persuasion – look at what works and what doesn't ▶ Practice analysis skills ▶ Practice research skills including an understanding of how to evaluate the reliability of sources	Students will select a method by which to inform the community about the issues and policies supported by candidates. They will defend one policy that they believe will bring about the most positive changes and align that policy with a specific candidate's position. Students may select from: ▶ Holding a debate with another student(s) open to the community ▶ Writing a detailed and convincing letter to the editor ▶ Creating a Public Service Announcement (PSA) ▶ Holding a workshop for community members ▶ Creating a series of three posters or a flyer convincing people of the "best" solutions for election problems These are a few ideas... as the service-learning project evolves others might surface.	Rubric (see page 29) Additional criteria (such as public speaking, writing, technology) may be added to the rubric once a presentation method (debate, PSA, letter, etc.) to inform people is selected.

"My 7th grade students are doing a service-learning project right now as part of the arthropod unit. They are applying their new knowledge and skills to test water quality and decide whether to release native salmon into a local stream. This unit, which I have taught for many years, has come to life. The kids are using what they have learned in class to help solve a real problem in their community."

— *Stephen Brown, teacher, Lisbon Central School, Connecticut*

Chapter 3:
Introduce Students to
Service-Learning

Define Service-Learning | Discover Needs/ Problems | Investigate Problems | Research Solutions | Decide on a Project | Plan the Project | Implement the Plan | Evaluate

Case Study: Improving Safety for Migrant Workers

Two representatives from the Vermont Agency of Agriculture, Food and Markets came to a Spanish class at Montpelier High School to discuss challenges facing the state's migrant workers. They explained that Vermont now has many Spanish-speaking dairy workers who help maintain dairy farms, and few of them know enough English to perform tasks safely.

Based on a specific need they had identified, the state Agriculture Agency representatives invited the students to create a CD for Vermont dairy producers who employ Spanish-speaking workers. The farmers could use the CD to help convey essential safety information in Spanish (since not all the workers can read).

The school's Spanish teacher recognized that this project fit well with the curriculum, helping students fulfill requirements for oral presentation, verb conjugation, conversational vocabulary and culture. Inspired to help, the students worked with the state Agriculture Agency to help alleviate communication barriers between dairy farmers and migrant workers and improve worker safety.

With help from the Vermont Migrant Education Association, the students began researching the needs of Vermont's migrant workers, listening to podcasts and reading newspaper articles. As students explored the complex dynamics of migrant labor, they learned about other problems the workers face, like low wages and limited access to health care.

After careful research, the students outlined their planned content for the safety CD and developed a two-month timeline that included weekly reflections and class progress reviews. They tracked their oral translations of written safety documents on fact sheets, which kept the class informed of each individual's progress and maintained the student enthusiasm and the classroom's collaborative spirit.

To produce their CD, students worked with the school's technology coordinator to learn Audacity software. When the CD was finalized, the students contacted local newspapers and wrote articles for the school's e-newsletter. The school community, impressed by the students' accomplishments, released a special edition of their e-newsletter; highlighted the project on a televised school board meeting; and included the project in the school's annual report.

The DOA distributed the CDs to dairy farmers across Vermont, but the confidentiality of recipients made it difficult for students to evaluate the effectiveness of their project. Despite this setback, the DOA assured students that they would monitor the impact the CD had on the health and safety of migrant dairy workers. Louise Waterman, Education Coordinator for the Vermont Agency of Agriculture, Food, and Markets, says that "this audio CD is a great tool for employees that are less able to read the printed words. It helps keep our farms safer for all employees. We look forward to working with the students on future projects."

"Every time that I do a service-learning project with my middle-school students I take time to build a collaborative environment within the group. The need for building positive relationships among students is extremely important in order for the work to go smoothly. This initial work pays off with huge dividends and sets the tone for the remainder of the school year."

— Stephen Brown, teacher, Lisbon Central School, Connecticut

Collaborate in the Classroom and Beyond

After considering your curricular objectives and deciding on an entry point, you're ready to introduce students to the KIDS Framework. The KIDS service-learning model (see page 14) has eight linear steps and five ongoing elements (the clouds) that teachers need to facilitate. This chapter introduces Step One of the KIDS Framework (Define Service-Learning) and two clouds (Collaboration and Reflection) that help create a classroom environment conducive to service-learning. While the KIDS service-learning model emphasizes student ownership, teachers play a critical role in creating a safe environment for students to learn new knowledge and skills and positively affect their communities. A warm and supportive classroom environment can foster better cognitive learning: research demonstrates that emotional and physical safety help the brain absorb and retain information.

Since student voice is critical to creating a meaningful service-learning experience, you'll need to foster a collaborative classroom environment that fully supports all student voices. Fostering a sense of teamwork and constructive communication will help students as they work together to generate ideas, explore options and forge community partnerships.

Students gain a strong sense of ownership for a project when they're included as equal partners from the beginning. The physical set-up of a classroom sends a powerful message to students about their partnership with each other and with you. For example, having everyone sit together in a circle facing each other can increase participation, respect and a sense of shared responsibility.

The initial activities in this chapter are designed to help students gain the skills needed to share their perspectives, learn to work in teams, and resolve conflicts. When students listen to each other and feel their opinions are heard, a cooperative team spirit marks their efforts. To create a collaborative environment, groups must take time to establish norms (shared principles or conventions) to guide behavior (see "Use GOILS to Develop Norms" on page 38 or use "The Being" in the Appendix on page 100). Individuals in groups need time to get to know each other before they can identify their needs with respect to group dynamics; depending on your student group, you may choose to use this activity a couple of weeks into the semester rather than at the outset.

Group norms often fall into categories, such as these adapted from the National School Reform Faculty:

Best	Safe	Fair
▶ Be fully present	▶ Support each other's learning with words, attitudes and actions	▶ Give everyone a turn *(side conversations are distracting)*
▶ If you wonder, ask	▶ Remember that we all learn in different ways	▶ Be inclusive
▶ Speak honestly	▶ Take care of yourself	▶ Start and end on time
	▶ It is okay to pass	▶ Be conscious of airtime
		▶ Give gentle reminders

Tool: Use GOILS to Develop Norms

As your group works to establish guidelines for collaborative work, a facilitator's tool known as GOILS (Groups of Increasingly Larger Sizes) can help to focus ideas and reach consensus. This exercise gives everyone involved a voice in the decision-making (unlike brainstorming, in which group members volunteer their ideas but not everyone may choose to speak).

1. Class members each write down five norms that they think are needed to work together successfully. It may be easiest for them to respond to a direct question like "What do you need to do your best work and learning in this setting?" Encourage concrete responses (e.g., "I need a chance to voice my opinion," rather than "I need to feel safe").

2. Once everyone has created a list, participants share their lists with a partner. From their two lists, each pair creates a list of five norms on which they agree.

3. Pairs then join up with other pairs, share their lists, and create a single list of five norms on which both pairs agree.

4. Continue this process until there are only 2-4 lists of five norms each.

5. Reconvene the whole group and have a spokesperson from each group report out one norm until all the norms are charted on a posted list (do not include exact repeats).

6. Reviewing the list as a group, encourage participants to ask questions about what ideas on the list mean; combine similar ideas; and reframe negative attributes into positive ones (e.g., "use encouraging words" rather than "avoid put-downs").

7. Use some method for determining consensus on the remaining group norms (e.g., thumbs up to mean "I agree with these norms and will work with them;" thumbs down to mean "I don't agree—more discussion is needed;" thumbs to the side to mean "I can live with these norms and will work with them"). If anyone can't agree to the list, ask them to explain why and offer another solution.

8. Post the final list to help remind participants of their shared agreement, and periodically reflect on whether your group process is adhering to these norms. (The Stoplight Check on Norms tool on page 39 provides an easy, visual means of completing this reflection.)

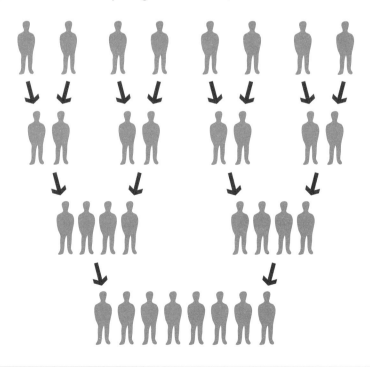

Once norms are established and the group has been working together for a while, circle back to discuss whether class members are following the established norms. The Stoplight Check on Norms tool that follows provides an easy, visual way to facilitate this discussion.

Tool: Stoplight Check on Norms

To complete this activity, you'll need a posted chart of class norms and small "dot" stickers in red, yellow and green. Posting the chart listing norms, invite participants to rate how well the group is doing by placing a single dot by each norm—choosing one of the three available colors.

▶ **A green dot** (a GO) means things are going well. It's a GO.

▶ **A yellow dot** (warning light) means we need to pay attention to this norm.

▶ **A red dot** (not being followed) means that we need to stop and talk about this norm.

After everyone has placed their dots on the chart, look over the chart together.

▶ What do class members notice?

▶ What things are going well?

▶ What norms need attention or further discussion?

Having students, teachers and community partners sit together in a circle can help to reinforce a spirit of collaborative partnership and shared responsibility.

Tool: Ways to Foster Collaborative Learning

During a service-learning project, one of the teacher's main jobs is to make sure all voices are heard and the class completes its work in a respectful and efficient manner. The following ideas can help you foster constructive relationships among students that enhance communication within and among groups. Consider your objectives and the needs of your students as you ask them to work in small or large groups.

Build Community and Resolve Conflict

▶ As a group, establish standards for respectful behavior in class that supports honest, supportive appraisal and discussion.

▶ Engage students in "low risk" ice breakers (see sample ice breakers in the Appendix on pages 101-102).

▶ Spend time working on group challenge games to foster teamwork skills. (See "Don't Spill the Beans" on page 42.) Be sure to include time for students to reflect on skills they have learned (e.g., listening, using positive language).

▶ Expect that groups will undergo predictable stages of growth and regression in their work together and coach them through those stages. In early stages, they may be anxious and uncertain, unclear of goals and expectations. As they begin organizing, there may be more overt conflict as team members vie for different roles or tasks. When group members commit to a task, they generally resolve these conflicts and begin working together more constructively.

▶ Create scenarios that portray difficult situations and have students practice positive communication and conflict resolution skills through role plays.

▶ Periodically reflect on how the group is doing as a community. (See Stoplight Check on Norms, previous page.)

▶ Mix up student groupings for various activities so they can experience different group dynamics.

▶ Have students reflect on different work styles and how they affect group work (see the Appendix on page 103).

Foster Constructive Group Process

▶ Have group members take on roles and responsibilities, such as leader, note-taker/recorder, reporter and time-keeper.

▶ As a group, create a project description (see page 66 for further guidance).

▶ Establish working committees, each with specific goals, tasks and timelines (see pages 73 and 74 for guidance on identifying tasks and timelines). While committees should confer with teachers regularly, the class needs to meet often as a whole to assess group progress and develop new tasks collectively.

▶ Offer feedback during group work by writing short notes to individual students, acknowledging what is being done well and providing suggestions.

▶ As a daily check-in tool (see Team Communication Check In Tool in the Appendix on page 104), consider using the following questions either with small groups of students or the entire class:

- Were all ideas heard?

- How are we treating each other?

- How are we doing as a team?

- Are we doing our best?

Participants can respond by holding up 0-5 fingers (with 5 being great), or by giving a thumbs-up/down/sideways signal. Another means of checking in is to have each student offer one word to describe how their team (or the class as a whole) is doing.

Organize for Learning

▶ **Brainstorming:** Set a time limit and encourage group members to generate a wealth of ideas through a brainstorming session. Everyone has a chance to talk and all ideas are recorded in writing (somewhere visible to the group) without any discussion of their merits. That discussion can occur once the brainstorming session is complete.

▶ **Carousel Group Exercise:** Hang easel paper on the walls, each labeled with a different topic. Small groups spend a few minutes brainstorming ideas on each topic, moving on to the next paper location when time is called.

▶ **Concept Map:** Organize or map ideas visually to demonstrate how they relate.

▶ **GOILS:** (see description on page 38). Start with individual lists of ideas, then have pairs form to discuss ideas. Those pairs then join other pairs, establishing consensus within larger groups.

▶ **Jigsaw:** Divide students into teams of 4-5 individuals. Each team member is assigned a different topic (e.g., topics A, B, C and D). Those with similar topics from each team (all the As, Bs, etc.) join up to form a work group and learn about that topic. Each person in the work group then returns to his/her original team to teach team members about the topic.

Election Project: Collaborative Environment – Don't Spill the Beans!

This activity would be done later in the project's development, perhaps before creating the project's action plan.

To help build their skills in planning, negotiation and collaborative problem-solving, the teacher challenges students with a complex team initiative called "Don't Spill the Beans." The students receive two coffee cans (one filled with beans, one empty), old bicycle tubing, and different lengths of nylon ropes. Using only these resources, their task is to transfer the beans from one coffee can to the other (not touching either can with their hands) without spilling any beans or knocking over the cans.

After students complete the task, they reflect on their experience. The teacher helps guide this process, asking: What helped you achieve your goal? What hindered your progress? What learning might you take from this activity and apply to your service-learning project?

Define Service-Learning

Early in the process, you'll want to explain to students what service-learning is and why it's a valuable means of acquiring both content knowledge and skills as well as helping the community. You can define service-learning at the outset, or suggest it as an approach to a problem or need that students have discovered. In either case, it may be helpful to consider the following ideas as you frame your conversation with students:

Students brainstorm ideas for the Effective Citizen activity.

▶ Explain that service-learning is more than just "community service," and offers an experiential means of shifting learning from the classroom into the community. (Share with students the KIDS principles or commonly confused terms from Chapter 1 as you review these concepts).

▶ Have students reflect on what it means to be an engaged citizen (see the Effective Citizen Brainstorm in the Appendix on page 105).

▶ Share examples of service-learning projects others have done (drawn from this guide, www.kidsconsortium.org, or local examples in your community). Consider inviting an experienced service-learning practitioner (whether teacher or student) to meet with your class, sharing stories and inviting questions.

▶ Have students define the terms "service" and "learning," and engage students in a game or activity to understand service-learning (KIDS Consortium has the "What Is It" game and other activities).

Value of Service-Learning

To help students understand the value of service-learning, you may want to discuss some of the background information highlighted in Chapter 1, summarized briefly here:

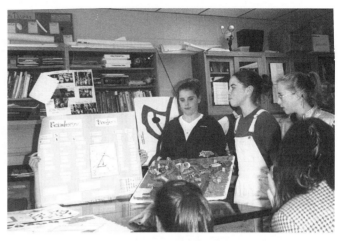

Students present their work to community partners.

▶ The world is changing rapidly and students today need to have skills that will help them adapt and excel as they encounter changing information, rapid technological advances and—often—not just multiple jobs but multiple careers. The world is very different than it was a generation or two ago and the "way we do school" should reflect that. Education can't operate under the old model of teacher as pitcher and students as empty cups, getting filled with all "the answers." Teachers don't have all the answers and students need skills, like problem-solving, conflict resolution, and critical thinking, that they can apply in many different contexts. Service-learning helps students acquire "21st century skills" that can improve their performance in school and in life.

▶ Service-learning builds valuable and enduring bridges with the community, fostering good relations that extend well beyond students' school careers. Students gain a deeper understanding of the community's needs and challenges, and may make valuable contacts that can help them in and beyond their school careers. The experiential nature of service-learning projects draws on multiple intelligences, and can help students find new strengths, gain confidence and become leaders.

▶ Service-learning, while still new to many teachers and students, is an established approach to meeting academic standards that is practiced in a growing number of schools and districts. There are now national standards for service-learning and the KIDS Framework reflects these standards, having been carefully refined to incorporate the experience of teachers and students across the country and beyond, some of whom have used the KIDS model for ten years.

Election Project: Define Service-Learning

The teacher divides the class into two groups and assigns one the word "service" and the other the word "learning." Each group brainstorms a list on the meaning of the word they received. The groups present their lists and invite additional ideas.

The teacher asks students to consider how they could bring "service" and "learning" into their classroom.

"One of the truly wonderful aspects of a service-learning project is the opportunity for students to genuinely reflect on what they have accomplished, and, more importantly, how it makes them feel. Reflections associated with service-learning help students process what they have learned, what could have been improved, and how they have made a difference—all lessons with lifelong applicability."

—*Glenn Nerbak, Portland High School, Portland, Maine*

Incorporate Ongoing Reflection

"There is only one thing more painful than learning from experience," Archibald MacLeish once wrote, "and that is not learning from experience." Throughout the discovery process (outlined further in the next chapter), and the rest of the service-learning project, students need to reflect critically on what they've learned and on the assumptions and conditions underlying their actions. Reflective activities can deepen their understanding of individual and cultural belief systems and their own patterns of behavior. Reflection activities stretch students into higher-order thinking, helping them become problem-solvers, better able to analyze and synthesize complex issues. To ensure that students experience both affective (feeling-related) and cognitive (academic-related) learning, reflection should occur before, during and at the conclusion of the service-learning process.

Activities can be targeted to individuals, small groups or entire classes. It may be appropriate to involve community partners in reflection activities as well. Choose varied activities that take into account

▶ students' developmental level;

▶ the purpose of reflection;

▶ the stage of the project; and

▶ the learning styles of participating students (see sidebar on Reflection Ideas for Multiple Intelligences).

Some of the products that students generate in the reflection process will be helpful as you work to document your progress over the course of the project. Chapter 6 provides more details on ways to record your progress (and prepare for final portfolios and presentations), but it can be helpful early on to consider the need for careful documentation.

"We don't learn from experience. We learn from reflecting on experience."

– *John Dewey*

Tool: Reflection Ideas for Multiple Intelligences

Linguistic
▶ Keep an ongoing journal

▶ Write a poem about your service work

▶ Write an article for the community newspaper that highlights your class accomplishments

Logical/Mathematical
▶ Identify a problem that you saw at your project site and devise a solution

▶ Construct a detailed timeline for the service project

▶ Compile data or collect information at the project site

▶ Explain how the scientific method pertains to your project

Bodily/Kinesthetic
▶ Create and perform a skit or a tableau

▶ Act out a possible television commercial that would encourage others to support your project's goals

▶ For the class, act without words the heart of your service-learning experience

Spatial
▶ Draw the place where you did your project

▶ Make a collage about your service project

▶ Create charts or maps to understand and explain your work

▶ Create a video that reflects what you have learned and accomplished during your service-learning project

Musical
▶ Compose a song that captures your service-learning experience

▶ Bring in a song that reflects your service-learning experience

▶ Notice the sounds and songs while you're working: what do you hear?

Interpersonal
▶ Have a small group discussion

▶ Share with one other person what you felt like before, during and after your service-learning experience

▶ Role-play a situation that you weren't sure how to handle

▶ Have your classmates role-play appropriate and inappropriate responses

Intrapersonal
▶ Write a journal describing your thoughts/feelings

▶ Create a drawing or painting that represents your feelings associated with the project

▶ Create a metaphor that exemplifies your thoughts about the project

Naturalist
▶ Create a web or flow chart that depicts the natural environment of your project

▶ Talk about, write about or role-play how the natural world was affected by your service-learning work

Credit: Amy Hediger

Tool: Reflection Questions

Learning:
▶ What did you learn? How might these lessons apply to other situations?

▶ What did you learn that you didn't know before?

▶ Did you learn what you thought you were going to learn?

▶ What is the most important thing that you learned?

▶ What academic skills did you use?

▶ What do you want to learn next as a result of your KIDS project/activity?

▶ How did you feel about doing the project?

Citizenship:
▶ How did your experience affect your sense of citizenship?

▶ What people were involved from the community?

▶ How do you think the community reacted to the project?

▶ What was your greatest contribution to this effort?

▶ How did your efforts make a difference?

Student Ownership:
▶ What was your part in the project?

▶ What will you remember about the project?

▶ What challenges did you face and how did you resolve them?

▶ What was your greatest challenge during this process?

Teamwork:
▶ What did you feel was the common goal of this group?

▶ In what ways did you work as a team, using the strengths of various group members?

▶ How did you feel about your team?

▶ What were the positive and negative elements of your group experience?

▶ What did you learn about yourself as a group member?

▶ What did you learn from the obstacles that you encountered?

▶ What did your team do well?

▶ What would you do differently another time?

General Process Questions:
▶ What was most meaningful about your project experience?

▶ What insights have you gained?

▶ What worked and what didn't work? What would you do differently?

▶ What did you like or dislike about the project?

▶ What was most helpful? Least helpful?

▶ How would you describe your experience to a student who knows nothing about service-learning?

Debriefing

After every activity, it's good to "debrief," giving students an opportunity to reflect on their experience and share observations about what they learned. That discussion can center on three questions:

▶ **What?** This involves a factual review of what occurred and what was accomplished.

▶ **So what?** Participants share their feelings and interpretation of the experience. Reflect on what students learned about themselves, others and the academic material. What difference did they make? Did they accomplish as much as planned? Why or why not?

▶ **Now what?** Where might students apply new knowledge in the project and in their lives? What do they need to plan/do/re-do/learn next?

Adapted from Islands of Healing: A Guide to Adventure-based Counseling by Jim Schoel, Dick Prouty and Paul Radcliffe. Dubuque, IA: Kendall-Hunt Publishing, 1995.

Debriefing gives students a chance to assess progress to date and plan for the next phases of the project.

Chapter 4:
Investigate Problems

Define Service-Learning　Discover Needs/ Problems　Investigate Problems　Research Solutions　Decide on a Project　Plan the Project　Implement the Plan　Evaluate

Case Study: Improving School Sanitation

Seventh-graders at the Lisbon Central School in Lisbon, Connecticut learned from the school nurse about a microbial challenge in their cafeteria. Noting that a recent policy change had influenced the cleaning of cafeteria tables, the nurse asked students to help determine the effectiveness of the current cleaner and cleaning procedures.

Students testing for microbes.

To learn more about this issue, students read two articles about the presence of microbes in public schools. They researched recommended cleaning protocol in public dining facilities. Then students devised a plan for observing the current cleaning practices in the cafeteria during each lunch period. Since all their data collection occurred in the cafeteria, students had to communicate routinely with the daytime custodian in charge of lunchroom cleaning. They also needed to secure permission from other teachers to miss classes that coincided with their scheduled lunchroom observations.

After collecting baseline data regarding the presence of microbes on cafeteria tables, students analyzed their findings. They realized that they needed to determine whether the current cleaner would be effective at microbe control if used properly (i.e., scrubbed on the tables versus wiped). Students conducted further controlled tests of table cleaning and used the resulting data to help generate proposed changes in policies and practices.

Some analysis of data (e.g., graph-making) occurred at home so that there would be adequate time in class for discussion and planning of next steps. Students presented their findings and proposed solutions to the school nurse, administrators, custodians and members of the school's allergy committee. Graphs prepared by the students and the subsequent discussion convinced school administrators to make changes in policies and procedures that would improve microbe control. "I think this project helped improve the sanitation of our school," one student noted while another observed "I'm proud that the work we did is helping keep students at our school safe and healthy."

Now that your students are familiar with service-learning and the KIDS Framework, you'll move along to the next two steps: Discover Needs and Problems; and Investigate Problems. This chapter will help your students explore needs and problems; research their history, causes and effects; and consider possible solutions.

Discover Needs and Problems

In Chapter 2, you considered your Entry Point to the service-learning process and means of facilitating Guided Discovery with students, helping them learn about community problems and needs. With that preliminary planning done, you're ready to engage students in Guided Discovery (choosing appropriate ideas listed on the right). The example on the following pages from the Election Project illustrates how the discovery process can unfold.

Tool: Guided Discovery

Guided Discovery is a facilitated process of inquiry through which students learn about school or community topics/needs/problems.

Walk through the school grounds or neighborhood with students, having them record (with a clipboard and camera) ideas for improvement.

Conduct a landscape survey to learn more about the history of the school grounds or neighborhood/ community park or public lands and its microclimate, soil and plant life, land uses and boundaries.

Students learn about a problem through a field survey with a community partner.

Use your town as text, conducting a community tour (by bus or foot), planned in conjunction with community leaders. Discuss with students and leaders what is special about the community. Identify current issues and needs.

Students tour a recycling facility to learn about waste issues.

Create a community map, identifying both positive and negative features, to help in brainstorming potential topics/needs/problems.

Organize a community fair, inviting agencies and organizations to bring displays that show their mission and possible topics/needs/problems. Students can practice their interviewing techniques, asking questions of organizational representatives.

Research community organizations by having students choose an organization or agency, find out about its mission and possible needs, and present their findings to the class.

Invite a guest speaker or panel of presenters who are working on relevant community issues.

Use literature and/or works of fiction to brainstorm topics/needs/problems.

Visit with students who are working on a service-learning project in another classroom or school to learn more about the process or a particular problem.

Have students interview local officials about challenges facing the community and how students might help address those needs.

Invite students to undertake a community survey involving citizens and/or local business owners to discover local topics/needs/problems.

Use a creative writing assignment to brainstorm possible topics/needs/problems.

Follow up on a compelling news story or letter to the editor. Sometimes a crisis—in the school or the local, state, national, or global community—can inspire action.

Have students use media of all kinds to identify topics/needs/problems.

Students interview seniors to discover their needs.

Election Project: Discovering Needs and Problems

In this example, the social studies teacher concluded that a "single topic" entry point would be the best means of engaging students in a service-learning project. The teacher sought to engage students in issues related to elections by facilitating the following activities:

▶ Several discussions in social studies class sparked student interest in the upcoming election. For one assignment, students read newspaper articles to learn more about the issues and discovered several state and local referendum questions of interest. They realized the importance of several local races and wanted to know more about candidates' positions on issues that concerned them.

▶ The teacher had a preparatory conversation with the Town Clerk to explore whether students might work on a service-learning project leading up to the next election. After sharing with the Town Clerk the concept of service-learning and highlights of the KIDS model, the teacher asked her to put together a one-page handout for students listing some issues regarding the upcoming election. The Town Clerk agreed.

▶ The teacher facilitated a pre-reflection with students, asking these questions: What do we know about the election? What do we still want to know?

Reflection

▶ Students then brainstormed a list of questions to ask the Town Clerk:

  • What do you do in the election process?
  • Who votes?
  • How many people vote in local elections? What percentage of voters vote? How does this community compare to others?
  • How are votes counted? Who counts them? How do all the precincts tabulate votes and communicate the results?
  • Are ballots printed only in English?
  • Do the voting machines malfunction?
  • What do you do after Election Day?
  • How does absentee voting work and who can do it?
  • What is the most challenging part of your job concerning elections?
  • What is the most rewarding part of your job concerning elections?
  • Why do you think people don't vote?
  • What do you to do to encourage people to vote?

▶ The class took a field trip to the Town Hall, meeting with the Town Clerk to learn how she and others in the community prepare for upcoming elections. The Town Clerk shared a handout with ideas for student involvement and engaged students in an activity designed to help them value their right to vote. Students returned to school and brainstormed a list of some issues on which they might work. They made journal entries describing their learnings and insights to date.

Election Project: Acknowledging Partners

Reflection

Dear Ms. Hernandez (Town Clerk),

Thank you for meeting with our social studies class at Town Hall last week. We learned a lot from your presentation, especially about voting trends, election laws, and registration procedures. We were surprised to hear that voter turnout has fallen steadily over the past thirty years. We talked this over in our class, after we returned to school, and we'd like to help the Town increase voter turnout this fall.

Your talk helped us understand how voting works and what we might do to help with voter turnout. We look forward to working with you on this important problem.

Sincerely,

The students in Ms. Smith's Social Studies Class

Brainstorm and Narrow Down Ideas

The Guided Discovery process typically leaves students with many ideas about the identified needs or problems. A short, timed brainstorming session allows students to generate and record these ideas without discussing their merits. Brainstorming engages students in creative and positive thought, encouraging them to think "outside the box" without having to think through all the ramifications of each idea. During the brainstorming, no one counters an idea or questions whether it is feasible or advisable. All ideas are recorded and—at the end of the timed session—the facilitator can check to make sure all participants understand the ideas that were shared. The class can then use the N/3 Prioritizing Tool (see below and election example on page 54) to narrow the list of ideas, and let students weigh in on which needs or problems interest them.

Tool: Focusing in through N/3 Prioritizing

Using the N/3 Prioritizing Tool helps students evaluate brainstormed ideas and note which they find most compelling. N/3 Prioritizing can be used any time a list needs to be narrowed, after brainstorming or other means of list creation.

▶ Combine similar ideas or merge complementary parts of different ideas to eliminate duplication.

▶ Divide the total number of ideas on the brainstormed list by three. Give each class member the resulting number of votes. For example, if the group brainstormed 18 ideas, then each group member would receive six votes.

▶ Give each class member six colored dots, and ask them to place the dots next to the idea(s) on the list that they like best. They may place as many of their six dots as they want to next to an idea.

▶ Once all the dots are assigned to ideas, it should be clear which idea(s) have the strongest support.

▶ If several choices receive high ranks, the group may decide to merge ideas or investigate multiple problems. (This latter option works well if students work in teams and have adequate teacher support for each team.)

Not all students may be enthusiastic about the topics the class has prioritized. To keep these students engaged, focus on other talents or interests they can contribute to the project (e.g., photography, video documentation, graphic or website design, community outreach, social media, construction planning, interviewing, writing, art, financial management, public relations, celebration planning, policy research, data collection, or logistics).

Students use a prioritizing tool to narrow down their ideas

Election Project: Narrowing Down Ideas

After meeting with the Town Clerk, the students brainstormed a long list of problems and concerns related to local elections. Their social studies teacher then invited students to use N/3 Prioritizing to select the most compelling problems from their collaboratively created list. Fifteen students identified 12 problems, casting 4 votes each for a total of 60 votes.

Based on their interest, indicated by a three-way tie, students decided to investigate further "low voter turnout," "lack of knowledge about local issues and candidates," and "not understanding the elections process."

Difficulty with elderly registration ✓
Low voter turnout ✓✓✓✓✓✓✓✓✓
People don't vote regularly ✓✓✓
Lack of knowledge about local issues and candidates ✓✓✓✓✓✓✓✓✓
Voter apathy ✓✓✓✓✓✓
Truth in advertising ✓✓✓✓✓
Absentee voting problems ✓
Technical problems ✓✓✓
Not understanding the election process ✓✓✓✓✓✓✓✓✓
Low voter trust in system ✓✓
Corrupting role of money ✓✓✓✓✓✓✓✓✓✓✓
People don't feel that their vote matters ✓✓✓✓

Investigate the Problem and Synthesize Research

Once students have identified problems of particular interest, they must gain a deeper understanding of each one so that the solutions they devise are informed and will address the problem. If, as a result of N/3 Prioritizing (see page 53), students select multiple problems of interest, teams of students can investigate the problem of their choice.

They can begin using a reflection activity (facilitated through a small- or large-group brainstorm) known as KWL—establishing what they already KNOW (or think they know); what they WANT or need to know about the problem; and how they will LEARN what they need to know (see Election Project: Using KWL to Investigate the Problem on page 55 and blank form in the Appendix on page 106).

To help focus their research, students may want to develop and answer a set of questions concerning the problem's evolution, causes and effects.

▶ **Causes** (What is creating the problem?)

▶ **Effects** (What impact is the problem having on people, property, environment, organizations, etc.?)

▶ **History/evolution** (When did the problem start? How has it changed over time? How have people addressed this problem in the past?)

▶ **Multiple perspectives** (What do different people/groups think about the problem? Is there agreement or disagreement about the causes and effects?)

To answer questions that arise during this phase of research, students need to seek information from both primary and secondary sources representing multiple perspectives. Teachers can facilitate this process by helping students identify appropriate people to contact, and ensuring that students know how to use the library, Internet and other resources. The Appendix entitled *Field Research*, on page 107 provides detailed guidance on helping students with primary and secondary research, and with conducting interviews, focus groups and surveys. At this stage, students can begin collecting quantitative and/or qualitative data about the problem. They will return to their initial (baseline) data after implementing their solution to help assess their impact on the problem/need and the community—Step 8 (Evaluate the Impact) in the Framework.

Students then need to refine their understanding of the problem, reflecting (through individual or group assignments) on what they've learned about the problem and why it matters to them. The following example on pages 56 and 57 demonstrates how the Exploring the Problem tool can be used to document research, facilitate the sharing of information, and help synthesize findings into a single location (a common document, bulletin board or class website). It's also useful for spotting discrepancies or conflicts between different research sources. This tool is useful for individual assessment as well, gauging knowledge gained by students in their research. A blank version of this tool is provided in the Appendix on page 110.

Election Project: Using KWL to Investigate the Problem

Students use KWL as a reflection tool to chart what they know, what they want to know, and how they will learn more about the problems they've identified. This process can help students identify baseline data they have about the problem/need and data they may need to collect.

What do we KNOW about the problems?

Problems:
▶ Low voter turnout (turnout is lowest among voters aged 18-29)
▶ Potential voters lack knowledge about local issues and candidates
▶ Potential voters do not understand the election process

What we know about the problems:
▶ Three state referendum questions on ballot this year—causing voter confusion
▶ Inaccurate campaign advertisements
▶ Limited time before voting day (November 4)

What do we WANT OR NEED TO KNOW about the problems?
(i.e., cause, effect and history)

▶ What election-related information do community members not know?
▶ What do they need to know?
▶ Election laws
▶ Offices up for elections and what those offices do
▶ Polling places
▶ Districting
▶ Types of elections
▶ Election calendar
▶ How does one get on the ballot?
▶ Initiative issues on this ballot?
▶ Who are the candidates?
▶ Referendum questions?
▶ Structure of municipal government
▶ Who is not voting?
▶ Who is registered?
▶ Voter trends for last election?
▶ Community makeup?
▶ Who are new residents?
▶ Can immigrants vote?
▶ Where are the gaps in government?
▶ Complaints about voting?

How will we LEARN what we want/need?

▶ Adults, school staff, other students, voters?
  Survey
▶ Rock the Vote
  Internet
▶ League of Women Voters
  Phone or Skype Interview
▶ Political parties
  Internet
▶ Community advocates
  Media/Newspaper/E-mail
▶ Policy makers
  Letters
▶ Town Clerk
  Visit
▶ Local candidates
  Discussion Panel

Election Project: Exploring the Problem

Directions: Use this set of questions to clarify what you know. Identify how you know what you know, using the modes of research labels listed below. For example, if you learned about the cause of a problem by interviewing someone, label it with the letter "I" for interview.

Modes of research:
Guest speaker: GS

Interviews: I

Survey: S
   Surveys could be secondary (e.g., use of existing data) or primary (e.g., student-generated)

Primary materials: PM

Secondary materials: SM

Problem:
Lack of knowledge about local issues, candidates and the voting process causes low voter turnout.

History:
When did the problem start? How has it changed over time? How have people addressed this issue over time?

✓ Voter turnout in our community has declined over the past 30 years. (GS-town clerk)

✓ In the elections of 1960, 1964, and 1968, voter turnout averaged 74 percent. In the elections of 2000, 2004, and 2008, voter turnout was 70 percent. (PM-town report 2009)

✓ The community bought new voting machines five years ago. (GS-town clerk)

✓ The town has started to allow elderly people to vote at nursing homes. (GS-town clerk)

✓ Thirty-five years ago, the voting age was lowered to 18. (SM-history text, We the People, p. 117)

✓ The civil rights movement helped change laws, making it easier for everyone to vote. (SM-history text)

Causes:
What leads to this problem?

Claim (the idea) & evidence (the information that indicates something is true)

Claim:
People have little or no faith in the system and the importance of voting.

Evidence:
Eric Plutzer, a political scientist at Penn State says "For many, voting is an unfamiliar task: They don't know where the polling place is, they may have no idea who represents them in the state legislature, and they're unlikely to have strong feelings about local issues such as school taxes or zoning." (SM-Charles Mindich, "Why Don't People Vote," 2006)

Claim:
People don't follow current events and so don't know the issues at election time.

Evidence:
"The decline in news consumption, which has taken place over the past four decades, has produced two generations of young adults who, for the most part, have barely an outline of what they need to make an informed decision in the voting booth." (SM-David Mindich, Tuned Out, 2004)

Claim:
Families aren't interested in discussing local or national issues politics at home.

Evidence:
Results from survey. (S-student created, administered, reviewed)

Effects:
What impact is the problem having on people, property, environment, organizations, etc.?

Claim:
A family habit of voting is passed on to kids.

Evidence:
Eric Plutzer, a political scientist at Penn State says, "If your parents are habitual voters, the chances of you voting before age 25 are much higher." (SM-Research Penn State: On-line Magazine of Scholarship and Creativity)

Claim:
Government is not representing all the people in our community when citizens do not vote.

Evidence:
"Some people argue that because nonvoters tend to be poorer, less educated and minorities, elected politicians can more easily disregard their interests when formulating public policy." (SM-Democracy in America, Annenberg Foundation)

Claim:
Special interests are gaining more power.

Evidence:
The Town Clerk observed in a town meeting the effect of one special interest group packing the hall with its members, effectively drowning out all other views. She used this to illustrate what she sees happening more often in local elections. (GS – Town Clerk)

Multiple Perspectives:
How do different people/groups view the problem? Do they agree or disagree about causes and effects?

The following claims come from the results of our survey, conducted between September 20 and September 23.

✓ Automated calls about candidates and issues are overloading and confusing potential voters.

✓ Negative campaign ads are making potential voters cynical so they "tune out" the elections process.

✓ Polls and media stories make potential voters feel like the election is a "done deal" and their votes don't count.

✓ Economic concerns are all-consuming, preventing voters from thinking about community concerns and civic responsibilities.

✓ Entertainment is winning out over information, and people aren't paying attention to news issues.

✓ Citizens have a responsibility to vote and many are shirking their civic duty.

Student Reflection on the Problem:
Lack of engagement in our governmental process, indicated by low voter turnout, stems from lack of knowledge about issues, candidates, and the voting process. The resulting poor representation in government harms the democratic process.

Works Cited:
Ginsberg Benjamin, Theodore J. Lowi, Margaret Weir. We the People, 7th Edition. New York: Norton, 2011.
Hernandez, (Town Clerk). "Voting and the Upcoming Election" presentation, September 19, 2011.
"The Maintenance of Democracy" in Democracy in America (Chapter 13). Annenberg Foundation, March 2006.
Mindich, David. Tuned Out: Why Americans under 40 Don't Follow the News. New York: Oxford, 2004.
Fergus, Charles. "Why Don't People Vote?"(An Interview of Eric Plutzer) in Research Penn State: The Online Magazine of Scholarship and Creativity (October 30, 2006).

Chapter 5:
Devise a Solution

Case Study: Promoting Sun Safety

Research Solutions

Decide on a Project

Create a Project Description

Public Relations and Celebrations

Reflection   Collaborative Environment   Public Relations   Celebration   Curriculum, Instruction and Assessment

Define Service-Learning   Discover Needs/Problems   Investigate Problems   **Research Solutions**   **Decide on a Project**   Plan the Project   Implement the Plan   Evaluate

Case Study: Promoting Sun Safety

Third-grade students at the elementary school in Eddington, Maine were surprised to learn that residents of their state have a higher risk of developing skin cancer than residents of many other states. To help address this problem, they decided to engage in a service-learning project focused on sun safety and skin cancer prevention. Students wrote a funding proposal and received a state agency grant to support their efforts.

To learn more about the problem, students met with the school nurse and talked to their parents and other adults. They did extensive research on how ultraviolet (UV) rays affect the body, and learned ways to prevent excessive sun exposure (such as wearing hats and sunglasses). Following their research, students brainstormed how they might address the problem.

They decided on a combination of three common and effective approaches—direct action, educational outreach and attempts to change policies (see Research Solutions on page 61). With their grant money, students purchased a protective hat for every third- and fourth-grader in their school. Students asked the school to routinely remind parents and students about the need for sun protection, and they provided recommendations on sun safety for the school newsletter.

Wanting to educate the larger community about sun safety, students formed a school wellness team and worked with local U.S. Department of Agriculture staff, as well as area hospitals and health organizations. With help from their partners, the students designed informational panel displays and brochures that they presented at local and state events. Students also did outreach in local daycares and preschools, offering tips on ways to reduce dangerous exposure to UV rays. They even made hats with large rims to share with younger students.

The Eddington School students drafted a sun safety policy (e.g., recommending sunblock and hats at recess and on field trips) for their school that the school board adopted. They then worked to implement similar policies throughout their school district and beyond.

Sun Safety students present their project as part of a Project Citizen Showcase at the Maine Statehouse.

Research Solutions

Once students thoroughly research and analyze their problem(s), they need to focus on ways to address the problem. During this part of the service-learning project, students will:

▶ set criteria for finding an effective solution (see page 62 for ideas);

▶ brainstorm multiple solutions;

▶ narrow down solutions to investigate; and

▶ gather the information necessary to judge each solution's merit.

The order of these steps may vary. At times it may make sense to start with criteria and then brainstorm solutions. If you're concerned this approach might restrict creativity, students can begin with a brainstorm and then use criteria to narrow down ideas.

It is best for students to consider a range of potential solutions, rather than concentrating too soon on one. Consider using the worksheet and activity provided in the Appendix (pages 111 & 112) to facilitate this process. If students become focused on one solution or type of solution, you can broaden their thinking by introducing different approaches to problems:

▶ direct work on the problem;

▶ education of others in the community; or

▶ attempts to influence decision-makers.

Often, students use a combination of these approaches.

Approaches to Service-Learning Problems

There are three action approaches students can take in addressing a problem, illustrated in the following sample problem.

Problem: Low voter turnout.

We work directly on the problem...
▶ Students arrange a voter registration drive.
▶ Students arrange transportation to the polls.

We educate others in the community to address the problem...
▶ Students write articles to the newspaper and talk with civic groups to raise awareness and get others to help with this problem.
▶ Students host a get-out-the vote party which features a debate between local candidates.

We influence appropriate decision-makers to address the problem
(see public policy box on page 64)...
▶ Students advocate with local officials to mail voting directions to all homes and to mandate the posting of voting directions at all polls.
▶ Students advocate with local officials to keep the polls open longer on election day.

DEFINE PROBLEM - - - - - ▶ **HAVE IMPACT**

WORK DIRECTLY EDUCATE COMMUNITY INFLUENCE DECISION-MAKERS

"We had a great solution—it just didn't fix our problem. We needed to do more research on who we should have been targeting. We gave our brochures to the wrong people."

-- High school student, Montpelier, Vermont

Working individually or in small groups, students research solutions and present the advantages and disadvantages of each to the entire class. On the following page is an example of the Comparing Solutions worksheet (see blank form in Appendix on page 113), which can be used to help students focus on the advantages and disadvantages of possible solutions. The tools for investigating problems (see Appendix on Field Research, page 107) can also be adapted to help students research the merits of solutions.

Students work in small groups to compare their ideas.

Tool: Developing Criteria for Evaluating Solutions

Developing criteria will help students:
▶ expand their thinking about possible solutions;

▶ narrow their focus on solutions to a problem; and

▶ recognize a good solution when they discover it.

Criteria can be created by students, provided by a teacher or community partner, or forged through some collaboration.

Example criteria:

Will the proposed solution have a positive IMPACT on the problem?

▶ How will the solution address the problem's cause(s)?

▶ Will the solution have a lasting impact?

▶ What are the solution's strengths?

▶ What are the solution's weaknesses?

▶ What kind of "approach to solving the problem" is it? (see box on page 61)

Is the solution FEASIBLE?

▶ Is there time to research, plan the solution and make an impact?

▶ Who are the community partners/experts that could help us?

▶ Who might support and/or oppose this solution?

▶ Do we have necessary funding?

▶ Can we get reliable information to affect this solution?

Will we learn NEW KNOWLEDGE and SKILLS?

▶ What will we learn?

▶ What skills might we acquire that would foster citizenship?

▶ How will greater knowledge of this topic enhance our academic studies?

▶ How might this project foster our sense of personal responsibility?

Do we CARE about this solution?

▶ Will developing this solution be both fun and challenging?

▶ Does it match our interests and passions?

▶ Can we make a difference?

Tool: Comparing Solutions

	Brief description of proposed solution: A "Get Out the Vote" Party		Brief description of proposed solution: B Bumper Sticker	
Criteria	**Advantages**	**Disadvantages**	**Advantages**	**Disadvantages**
IMPACT	According to Eric Plutzer, many people are uninformed about where to vote, who represents them, and what the issues are. This solution will help educate voters on all these factors. Our survey confirmed what David Mindich's book Tuned Out: Why Americans under 40 Don't Follow the News says about people not knowing the issues at election time.	Some students are concerned that people who really need information about voting and the issues would not attend.	There's a widely held belief bumper stickers do have some power to get people to think.	There's no empirical evidence showing that bumper stickers change behavior, according to Patti Brown, graduate researcher of political advertising. Lasting impact? Passive and indirect approach, similar to efforts that have been tried, but that are not doing much to help. Short message provides little to no means to educate people on the elections process.
FEASIBILITY	TIME: We have 6.5 weeks before November elections to complete the project. FUNDING: The town's community centers have agreed to loan their space free of charge; total supply cost is within our $200 budget. COMMUNITY PARTNERS/ EXPERTS: Town Clerk is already helping us and candidates are available for the dates we picked.	Principal is concerned about transportation to and from this event because it would happen at night. Getting the word out about this event could be challenging	TIME: The high school vocational graphic arts program can make bumper stickers in four days from the time we give them the design. FUNDING: We can have 500 printed for $250. COMMUNITY PARTNERS/ EXPERTS: Our art teacher is willing to help us with a design. The director of the vocational graphics arts program is giving us a break on the price, and she is willing to have her students help us, too.	Creating bumper stickers may not involve many students in a real way. We'd just give a design to the vocational center. We could each design a sticker and have a contest for the one we use, but after the contest there still would be little student involvement.
NEW KNOWLEDGE & SKILLS	Social Studies course objectives met: The election process, researching primary and secondary sources, analysis of candidates, issues and policies. ELA skills: interviewing, evaluating websites/ sources, argumentation, and presentation.		ELA: connotation & denotation, puns, paradoxes, double entendre, abstract vs. concrete nouns, parts of speech, persuasion, argument, rhetorical devices & strategies SS: propaganda, political slogans Graphic Arts: messaging, iconography	
CARE	We're not just reading about the problem or listening to adults talk about it—we're bringing people together to think about and discuss the issues. In addition, we're informing and teaching people about the election process.	Some classmates are more interested in doing the interactive theatre skits.	We're not just reading or listening to adults talk about the problem. Making designs to tell people why they should vote is creative and fun.	
OTHER?	We're a pretty big group, and there will be a lot to do to keep us all busy.			We are a pretty big group, and once the design is done there wouldn't be much left to do.

What Is Public Policy and How Is It Made?

Public policymaking is the process by which those involved in governing bodies make decisions and foster certain actions. Policies typically evolve from the ongoing dialogue among those who demand change, those who make decisions, and those who are affected by the policy in question.* Within the context of service-learning projects, students should be aware that governing bodies create policies that affect their problem or topic. Examples of governing bodies are school administrations, school boards, city and town councils, state and national legislatures, and governmental agencies.

As people in communities identify problems and formulate possible solutions, they may turn to government for support. The policymaking process gives people with different opinions a chance to discuss their concerns and weigh potential solutions. The process typically requires extensive research (collecting and analyzing data about the efficacy of different solutions), and strong advocacy (with those invested in a particular solution arguing its merits). Some public policies are written into laws by elected legislators. Other policies are outlined in rules and regulations drafted and carried out by state and federal agencies.**

Public policies have a broad impact on the way we live our lives—affecting our individual rights, our economic status, our natural environment, and the well-being of our communities. Citizens can be involved at all levels of the policymaking process, taking action in any of the following ways and more:

▶ attending public meetings;

▶ writing to elected representatives and newspapers;

▶ making phone calls to elected officials and other concerned citizens;

▶ monitoring legislative proposals;

▶ participating in demonstrations;

▶ encouraging other citizens to support particular initiatives;

▶ conducting research;

▶ learning about issues and candidates and making informed votes;

▶ working with elected officials to create proposals; and

▶ testifying at public hearings.**

*Adapted from Larry N. Gerston's Public Policymaking in a Democratic Society: A Guide to Civic Engagement (Armonk, NY: Center for Civic Education/M.E. Sharpe, 2002).

**Adapted from Project Citizen (Calabasas, CA: Center for Civic Education, 1996).

Students can build greater awareness of service-learning and its merits through presentations to adult committees and boards.

Decide on a Project

This step in the service-learning process provides an opportunity to increase student ownership and apply critical thinking and collaboration skills. Students need to choose their solution carefully as it will become the basis for designing and implementing their service-learning project. One way to approach this task is to use a decision-making matrix (see the following Election Project example and blank form in the Appendix on page 114). Students use criteria on the y-axis to compare possible solutions on the x-axis. There are multiple ways to use the decision-making matrix. Individuals can rate it and bring it back for group consensus. Students can work in small groups, rating each solution or criterion using information collected and analyzed during their research. The solution with the highest total score may be the most practical and effective approach. If problems or needs are too large for students to feasibly address in entirety, students should identify solutions that address a portion of the problem or need.

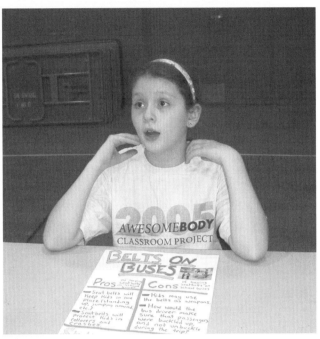

A student explains the pros and cons of a possible solution.

Election Project: Using the Decision-Making Matrix

Four groups of students each rated one solution on a scale of 0-5 all criteria (with 0 being least effective and 5 being most effective). The class then discussed the ratings and merged them into a final chart:

	Bumper sticker	Interactive theater	Door-to-door	Get out the vote party/ debate
Impact	1	3	4.5	5
Feasibility	4	2	1	4
New knowledge and skills	1	5	5	5
Care	3	2	4	5
Total Points	9	12	14.5	19

Create a Project Description

Drafting a written project description can help students identify key elements of their project.

Service-learning groups often function best when they develop a project description, which pulls together preliminary research and planning into a written statement that can help focus students throughout the project. The description should identify:

▶ the problem or need and why it is important;

▶ the chosen solution;

▶ names of participating community partners; and

▶ the positive impact students hope to achieve.

Writing project descriptions as a whole class can be difficult. Consider asking students to write key phrases, ideas or words to include and then have a small group of students draft a description using those terms, bringing it back to the entire class for revisions and adoption.

In addition to guiding students as they move through the project, the project description can be adapted into press releases and other media materials used to communicate with the community about what students are seeking to do.

Election Project: Developing a Project Description

Project Description:

We plan to host a fun and informative "Get Out the Vote" party at two community centers—with a candidate debate and students distributing voting information. These gatherings are designed to offer a comfortable, informative setting that gets community residents more interested in local issues and more motivated to vote, combating the current low voter turnout. To do this event, we will partner with the community centers, local election officials, candidates and local businesses (who may help sponsor the event). We hope this effort will lead to at least a 10 percent increase in our community's voter turnout on November 4.

Public Relations and Celebrations

Once your class has set the course for its service-learning project, it's time to consider how to engage the community and celebrate milestones with community partners. As you look at each phase of your project (early, middle and late), consider the best means of sharing progress updates within and beyond the school community. There may be natural transition points that lend themselves to celebrations, giving students a chance to acknowledge their progress and appreciate their partners. While some opportunities for public relations and celebration may arise spontaneously, it's helpful to plan these elements from the outset.

Invite students to brainstorm a list of ways to inform and engage the public, school community and policy-makers in their service-learning project. To generate media attention at various stages of their project, students may want to draft and distribute a news release to school and local newspapers, community websites and radio and television stations. Consider making use of social media forums such as Facebook and Twitter and/or setting up a blog. The news release should include clear contact information and give a brief, factual account of what is occurring (including the five W's: who, what, when, where, and why—see Election Project Press Release below). If possible, identify the name of the desk editor at each media outlet to get the attention of the right person. Try to include a hook, something to whet the interest of the reporter. Keep the release to one page and put it on school letterhead.

Election Project: Publicizing Events

Public Relations

October 5, 2010
Contact: Andrea Smith
asmith@aos.577.edu
207-123-4567

FOR IMMEDIATE RELEASE

Students Host Get-Out-the-Vote Party and Debate at Two Local Community Centers

On Thursday, October 14, from 6:00 p.m. to 8:00 p.m. (see attached schedule), students from Main Street School will host their first "Get-Out-the-Vote" Party featuring

- a debate among five candidates running for local office;

- an informal party and open discussion with candidates after the debate;

- voter registration information tables; and

- information regarding issues on the November ballot.

As part of a service-learning project, local students will host two interactive "Get Out the Vote" parties at local community centers—the first at the Main Street Community Center on October 14 and the second at the South Street Community Center on Thursday October 21 (from 6-8 p.m.). "These events are designed to offer a comfortable setting for community residents to learn about local issues," explains Isabel Sorrento, a student at Main Street School. "We worked hard to plan this event and hope it will raise voter turnout locally by 10 percent." In creating the evening program, students collaborated with community center partners, local election officials, candidates and local businesses.

Students expect a large turnout for both events. Both the Middle and High School Jazz Bands will perform during the evening.

More information on the two evening events is available on the school website: www.mainstreetschool.edu/events/voteparty.html.

"Our national study of the impact of service-learning on youth participants yielded some surprising results. One was that celebration was actually negatively correlated with outcomes. We dug more deeply into this issue by talking with students. Students told us that when they participated in service-learning, they felt that they were addressing real community problems and becoming part of the "solution." The celebrations were interpreted as being nice, but made them feel like they were involved just to win a prize, like a pizza party. In our words, it appears as though we moved them from intrinsic motivation or wanting to be engaged in service in order to make a difference, to extrinsic motivation or wanting to be engaged because there was a reward at the end. This one was an easy fix. If you explicitly link demonstration of impact to celebration of the impact, then the correlations became positive."

— *Shelley H. Billig, Ph.D., Vice President, RMC Research Corporation, Denver, CO*

Small celebrations at each project milestone can help sustain students' enthusiasm. These celebrations are not simply parties or rewards; they are authentic demonstrations of student work and help students integrate what they have learned and share that knowledge with others. See the Ways to Celebrate sidebar on the following page for some common ways that classes acknowledge their service-learning achievements.

Election Project: Celebrating Accomplishments — Celebration

Students invited the Town Clerk, their principal, the district superintendent and available teachers to a Brown Bag Lunch at their school during their lunch break. They informally presented their project description and asked for feedback and support. They recorded their conversation with a digital camera and later used clips to announce and promote the Get-Out-the-Vote party.

Be sure to invite community partners to any project celebration and have students regularly acknowledge their contributions through letters (to the partners and to local papers), project scrapbooks, celebratory gatherings, and other creative means. Community partners often devote a great deal of time and in-kind support to projects, and they appreciate having their contributions recognized, not just within the school—but within the larger community. Plan ways of acknowledging their support that provide the kind of visibility they deserve.

> JUNE 8, 2000
>
> Dear Laura Neman,
>
> Thank you for locating Amy and Tom. I'm glad you did because we needed them to make a map so we could locate trees and plants we didn't want to cut down. We thank you for giving up your time to be with us and for always being there. We also want to thank you for getting people and classes involved. Thanks for getting donations for tools and materials. Thanks for helping us get the property we needed to build the trail. I hope you come back next year to help the rest of the trail. I'll be there next year when you need me.
>
> From,
> Brook

Ways to Celebrate

▶ **Ribbon-cutting** or opening events (with speakers, tours, music and refreshments) for projects involving construction or renovation of some facility

▶ **Presentations** to school committees or town councils, reporting on project findings and recommendations

▶ **Public forums or presentations** sharing student learnings with interested community members

▶ **Displays of student work** (in community spaces such as a town hall or library)

▶ **Awards for outstanding effort**—going to students, community partners or both. Students can make the awards themselves or nominate community partners or their projects for state or local service awards (see more at www.student-service-awards.org)

▶ **Participate in regional or national service-learning celebrations** such as the KIDS Consortium annual Student Summit for participating schools throughout New England.

Chapter 6: Plan and Implement the Project

Case Study: Speak Out for Understanding

Plan the Project

Identify Tasks and Resources

Election Project: Tasks and Resources

Create a Timeline

Election Project: Action Plan with Timeline

Document the Project

Sidebar: Means of Documenting Projects

Implement the Plan

Sidebar: Reflection Opportunities

Election Project: Student Planning Sheet

Sidebar: Safety Considerations

Sidebar: Take Care of Yourself

Sidebar: Trouble Shooting

Evaluate the Project's Impact

Election Project: Evaluate the Project's Impact

Define Service-Learning   Discover Needs/ Problems   Investigate Problems   Research Solutions   Decide on a Project   Plan the Project   Implement the Plan   Evaluate

Case Study: Speak Out for Understanding

Special needs students at Harwood Union High School in South Duxbury, Vermont realized that most students at their school did not understand the challenges that people with disabilities face. Few students understood the complications and challenges of living with a physical, social, or learning disability, nor did they recognize how stressful and frustrating others' reactions could be.

A teacher invited a guest speaker from the Vermont Parent Information Center (VPIC) to join the class of special needs students to discuss with them the challenges and rights of students with disabilities. Following that discussion, the students decided—in cooperation with their teacher and the school's speech-language specialist—to address the lack of understanding within their school community through a service-learning project.

Collaborating with their community partner, VPIC, students explored websites and other sources to learn more about the problems and legal rights of those with disabilities and what could be done to

improve challenges within school settings. Incorporating fundamental learning skills outlined in the Vermont State Education Standards, students practiced critical thinking, problem solving, communication, citizenship, and personal goal-setting. They researched their disabilities using their own educational records. As the project unfolded, students kept portfolios or notebooks in which they reflected on their individual and class progress, as well as their feelings.

Based on their research and reflections, students concluded that it would be helpful to provide more information to members of their school community about the challenges that people with disabilities face in the educational system. They decided to create a documentary about their own experiences and an accompanying teacher's guide, being sure to include a spectrum of disabilities. The students filmed interviews with each other and members of the student body. They questioned teachers about their observations of students with disabilities in the classroom. The class celebrated their accomplishments by airing their film for the school community.

Following the video presentation, comments from teachers, students, parents, and community groups provided evidence that their project had increased understanding. The video and educational pamphlet generated valuable school-wide dialogue, and increased the social connections between students with and without disabilities. Equally important, the students with disabilities found that they were better able to communicate with others about their disability and advocate for appropriate accommodations at their school.

To learn more, please visit: http://speakoutforunderstanding.pbworks.com/w/page/17619161/FrontPage

Plan the Project

Now that your students have developed a project description, they're ready to get organized and implement their solution. The next three steps of the KIDS Framework require collaborative planning among teachers, students and community partners—making sure everyone involved understands the work plan and timeline. This chapter helps you attend to all the essential elements of project planning, implementation and evaluation:

▶ tasks and roles;

▶ resources, skills and information needed;

▶ establishing a timeline;

▶ documentation;

▶ essential safety precautions;

▶ data collection and analysis; and

▶ evaluating the project's impact on the community.

Identify Tasks and Resources

Students need to determine what's required to accomplish their project and what roles their community partners may play. They can begin by brainstorming a "to do" list of tasks and noting what resources (e.g., contacts, skills, information) are needed to complete them. After compiling a thorough list, students can determine the appropriate order for completing tasks and assign roles and responsibilities. As the project progresses, they can add, change or delete tasks as needed.

Election Project: Tasks and Resources

Tasks (prioritized, with 1 being the most immediate need)	Resources
• Create information sheet (4) • Develop list of contacts (2) • Talk with community center officials (3) • Contact business owners about donations (3) • Plan and arrange audiovisual needs (5) • Plan the party (5) • Assign tasks (1) • Buy supplies (7) • Send out invitations (6) • Set up party (9) • Have party (10) • Clean up from party (10) • Contact community members to participate (3) • Contact candidates (3) • Contact local media (8) • Prepare news release (7) • Develop post survey for after get-out-the-vote party (8) • Conduct survey (11) • Analyze survey results (12) • Meet with town clerk after election to discuss project's impact (12)	Library Town Clerk Community center directors Local business association Audiovisual club manager Candidates Local newspaper, TV, and radio stations Internet

"We came up with a map, breaking down the land into zones for the students to study. Every zone had a student historian, scientist, mathematician, poet, writer and surveyor. In all our classes, in an integrated manner, we started turning to the kids and saying 'okay, what do we need to accomplish?' From that point on, the kids really took over the project. Every student went in there with a job to do, knowing that his or her part was one segment of the whole... Then they came back to school to refine their writings and to prepare a document that would be the pool of our work for that day."

— *Eighth-grade teachers at Lewiston Middle School*

Create a Timeline

Once tasks and resources are identified, students, teachers, and community partners can map out weekly and daily action steps. The Election Project timeline shown below provides one possible format. Using this chart as a guide, students could break into teams, with each team deciding what specific tasks are required, how they will accomplish them, and who is responsible for what (see Student Planning Sheet on page 77 and a blank form in the Appendix on page 116). Team structures help students be accountable to one another (see the Team Communication Check-in in the Appendix on page 104). Timelines can be posted in the classroom, on a school bulletin board, or in class website, so students and teachers can track progress throughout the project. Timelines can also be depicted graphically (see Election Project example below and blank form in the Appendix on page 115).

Election Project: Action Plan with Timeline

Objective	Tasks and Activities	Persons Responsible	Completion Date	Status
Contact community partners	Develop list of contacts from Town Clerk and local business association	Haley's group	September 10	made lists 9/8
Plan party	Contact community members, center directors, and candidates	Diego's group	September 24	contacts made 9/22
Evaluate impact of project on community	Develop post-survey for after get-out-the-vote party	Lucas and Jacob	October 7	created 10/5
	Conduct survey	Lucas and Jacob	October 25	
	Analyze survey results	Binh's group	October 28	
	Meet with Town Clerk after election to discuss project's impact	whole class	November 16	
Publicize event	Work on information sheet	Isabel's group	September 28	drafted 9/23 revised 9/27
Host party	Plan A-V needs for party	Aadi and Bruce	September 18	arranged 9/17
	Send final info to candidates	Ellen and Chi	October 5	mailed 10/3
	Contact media, send out press release and invitations	Elizabeth's group	October 3	mailed 9/28
	Pick up supplies	Lucas and Jacob	October 20	picked up 10/18
	Set up for party at community center	whole class	October 20	
	Host party and cleanup	whole class	October 21	
	Arrange for rides home at 8 pm	whole class	October 21	
Reflect and celebrate	Invite Town Clerk in after the party	Juliana and Tai	October 27	called 10/15- will call to confirm 10/26
	Create questions for us to reflect on as a class	Juliana and Tai	October 15	
	Plan AV equipment to record reflections	Aadi and Bruce	October 27	done October 11
	Contact Town Clerk after the election to see results and invite her in to discuss	Juliana and Tai	November 11	
	Reflect on our impact	whole class	November 21	

Election Project: Action Plan with Graphic Timeline

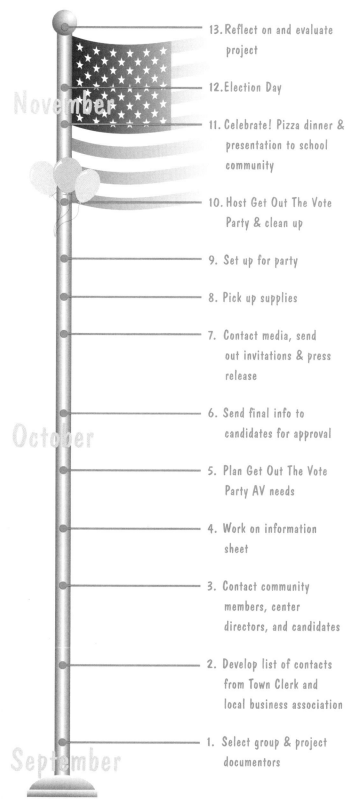

November

13. Reflect on and evaluate project

12. Election Day

11. Celebrate! Pizza dinner & presentation to school community

10. Host Get Out The Vote Party & clean up

9. Set up for party

8. Pick up supplies

7. Contact media, send out invitations & press release

6. Send final info to candidates for approval

October

5. Plan Get Out The Vote Party AV needs

4. Work on information sheet

3. Contact community members, center directors, and candidates

2. Develop list of contacts from Town Clerk and local business association

1. Select group & project documentors

September

Document the Project

Fully documenting every phase of the service-learning project helps students prepare project portfolios, organize final celebrations, share, and evaluate their accomplishments. Students need to discuss how they will maintain a thorough record of the evolving project—taking photographs, field notes, and video, as well as keeping track of phone calls, meetings, and other key events. If students work in teams, one group may take the lead in documenting the effort, compiling appropriate materials over the course of the project. Many classes use group websites or three-ring binders to collect and organize project materials. Teachers and community partners also need to collect and save items such as project work plans or matrices for assessment. The Means of Documenting Projects sidebar (see page 76) lists materials that many service-learning participants collect. The Appendix includes a blank Project Brief (see page 117) that can be used to help document your project.

Students take notes about their field observations.

Implement the Plan

Once students have outlined the tasks involved in their project, they can begin putting their plan into action. At this stage, the class often breaks into small groups charged with specific tasks. These groups give students an opportunity to get more deeply engaged in decision-making, as each "working committee" shapes a "group action plan" with specific goals, tasks, and timelines. When small groups begin working together, it can be helpful to revisit the group norms previously established (see pages 37-39).

Students may want to use the Student Planning Sheet (see the following Election Project example and blank form in the Appendix 116) as they determine what steps are needed to accomplish their tasks, who will do what, and when they will complete steps. Teachers need to consider learning objectives and group dynamics as they decide how to break students into groups and assign tasks.

Each working committee can report on progress at an all-group meeting (held weekly or as needed). Progress monitoring, one of the National Standards for Service-Learning (see www.nylc.org), engages students in collecting evidence from different sources, demonstrating how they are meeting their service-learning goals. This ongoing process of gathering data and reporting on progress helps students refine their service-learning project, accomplish high-quality work, and assess their impact at the end of the process.

Many teachers ask students, parents, and an administrator to sign the Student Planning Sheet. These signatures help to ensure student ownership, parent acknowledgment of tasks, and administrative support for the project. Establishing this clear understanding at the beginning builds a solid foundation for the project and supports each student's involvement.

Means of Documenting Projects

Written materials:
▶ short project description and timeline;

▶ a record of the number of teachers and students participating; grade levels; schools involved with a contact name/phone and e-mail at each school

▶ documentation of student ownership (i.e., what decisions did students make and how did they make them? what tools or techniques helped facilitate the process?)

▶ a description of how the project was chosen, what community issues/needs were addressed and who the community partners were

▶ a description of the links between project activities, state standards and assessments used

▶ evidence of student work that shows mastery of new learning

▶ teacher reflections about the project's successes and challenges; what might be done differently next time; what means of assessment were used and why; what changes at the community or school district level would better support service-learning; and what might be done to institute such changes

Attachments:
▶ photos, videos and a project web page (if available)

▶ examples of student reflection/journals, products, artifacts from performances and project assessments

▶ student-written articles and letters

▶ local press coverage

▶ interviews, anecdotes, comments and quotes from teachers, students, school administrators and community members

▶ statements or presentations made about the project to the school, civic or professional groups (including any video and audio tapes); and documents or agendas from meetings

Election Project: Student Planning Sheet

Project name: _Get out the Vote Party & Debate_

Group name and members: _Contact candidates —Diego, Juliana, Elizabeth, Binh_

Group objective: _Write a letter that explains the party/debate idea to local candidates and requests their participation in the debate_

We will be assessed on: (product and process) _Letter, business skills_

We will help the community by:
Getting information out so people understand issues and are more motivated to vote. The community meets candidates and learns how to use voting machines.

Tasks:

What?	Who?	By When?
Get a list of candidates/addresses	Elizabeth	September 8
Divide list among group	All	September 9
Write drafts, peer edit and revise	All	September 13
Teacher conference/edit	Ms. Smith	September 15
Final draft and send	All	September 18
Follow-up phone calls	All	September 22

What will we learn: _How to write a business letter using persuasive language_

What resources will we need: _computer, Community Center Director_

Elizabeth Hall	_Gabriela Nunez-Hall_	_Ms. Smith_
Student	Parent	Administrator

Date: _September 6, 2010_

Reflection Opportunities during Plan Implementation

▶ Compare what your expectation was with what's happening
▶ Reflect on the process, norms
▶ Reflect on the project
▶ Reflect on their own learning

Safety Considerations

▶ Complete parent permission/release forms and student health forms (providing clear indications of student allergies and other potential health issues). Forms should include emergency contact information.

▶ Develop contingency plans for weather-related and other emergencies, as well as procedures for dealing with medical emergencies.

▶ Make sure that any plans for travel beyond school grounds meet school district transportation requirements.

▶ Check liability insurance for community partners and for the school (e.g., to cover drivers).

▶ Plan adequate supervision.

Adapted from Service-Learning and School Improvement in New Hampshire: Learning from the Field.

Take Care of Yourself by Pamela Toole, Ph.D.

As we support, mentor and learn from young people who are making a difference in their communities, it's easy to forget one of our most important roles—modeling enthusiasm for work alongside a healthy capacity for self-care. Service-learning is a pedagogy that connects to the real world, which is inherently unpredictable and can be problematic and stressful. As we navigate these challenges with students, they look to us to model a sense of life balance and demonstrate self-renewal in the midst of demanding work. They want to see teachers and mentors successfully juggle the pressures of day-to-day life and classroom projects with grace, humor and minimal stress.

As a practitioner of service-learning, you need—as Mother Theresa observed—to keep putting "oil in your own lamp," both personally and professionally, to successfully light the way for others. You can best serve your students by sustaining your own health and life balance (something the institutions we work for and with don't always support). Consider cultivating practices that will help renew you on many levels: inner self/spiritual (prayer, meditation, journaling); creative self (art, music, dance); physical self (exercise, nutrition, humor); and communal self (relationships, support circles, nature). Professionally, attending a conference or observing the work of another teacher can help recharge one's passion for teaching. Investing time in renewing practices will reinvigorate your teaching and help students find healthy ways to manage stress in our demanding, 24/7 world.

Pamela Toole, Ph.D., is currently the vice-president of Compass Institute and formerly directed the Professional Development Department at the National Youth Leadership Council (NYLC). She has led service-learning workshops for educators in over 40 states, many involving mentoring and peer education programs.

Trouble Shooting

It's important to remember that unforeseen challenges are an inevitable part of the process. With guidance and support, students can learn to see obstacles as learning opportunities rather than as problems. It may be helpful to revisit with students some of the tools provided in Chapter 3, particularly the Stoplight Check on Norms (page 39) and Ways to Foster Collaborative Learning (page 40). Here are some additional means for dealing with challenges that a group may encounter:

Class loses energy
- Set a deadline for each aspect of the project to help maintain momentum.
- Have a periodic group check-in to discuss frustrations and successes.
- Make sure the project is timely and addresses a need that students find compelling.
- Celebrate small successes and review what is working well.

Student interest diminishes
- Invite students to identify where problems are arising and why.
- Develop ongoing means of group assessment, with frequent check-ins and nonjudgmental discussion.
- Check the class norms or "Being," or do other team-building exercises (see Chapter 3 for suggestions).
- Remind the class that all projects have a natural ebb and flow.
- Student interest survey to connect to goals of project.
- Remind students of the project's purpose (review the project description).
- Determine where the obstacles lie—whether in content (facts, concepts, skills); process (instruction and the way students make sense of the content); or product (how students demonstrate what they have learned).

Group conflict
- Remember that some conflict is a healthy part of group process and help students to figure out how they will work together (see Chapter 3 for further resources).
- Determine whether students have some pre-conceived ideas about a problem or solution that may be blocking their ability to move forward as a group.
- Ask students what is going on and tell them what you are observing (without making judgments).
- Step back and review the students' "project description" to inspire cooperation.
- Introduce students to win/win conflict resolution techniques.

Disruptive students
- Have students review the established class norms (see Chapter 3).
- Check to make sure that students understand their role and the context of the larger project. Are groups small enough and structured in a way so that the actions of each individual matter?
- Discuss whether students have enough to do or—alternately—feel overwhelmed by tasks that seem too large and complex.

- Has the project team discussed and agreed on constructive behaviors? Refer back to the group contract or guidelines reached during early team-building work (see Chapter 3).

Unsupportive colleagues
- To make sure that teachers have meaningful roles and a sense of ownership in the project, try to link aspects of the project to colleagues' special interests.
- Build in administrative approval on the project planning form.
- Inform colleagues and administrators of progress and forewarn them of any potential inconveniences resulting from the project.
- Invite colleagues into the class to observe and participate so they can witness firsthand the students' excitement.

Tensions with a community partner
- Meet with the community partner at the outset to discuss each party's interests, roles and expectations.
- Invite community partners into the classroom.
- Keep community partners informed.
- Publicize the role of community partners and routinely acknowledge their contributions.

- Celebrate accomplishments throughout the project.
- Decide on a mode of communication that works best for both parties (i.e., e-mail versus phone).
- Invite community members to reflect with students on what is working well and what needs to be improved.

Inadequate funds
- Develop a fundraising plan with students that may involve special events, sales, or proposals to schools or community foundations for grant funding.
- Consider what the community might donate in terms of time, talent and materials.
- Encourage students to write letters, make fundraising contacts, and apply for grants—helping them practice effective communication skills.

Inadequate supervision
- Encourage students to produce a newsletter or article that explains the project and outlines their need for volunteers.
- Contact parents, a local college, a service organization, and/or a senior association and develop a list of volunteers who can be mobilized through a phone tree.

- Request that your school or district hire a volunteer coordinator.

Transportation complications
- Schedule bus transportation early to avoid potential conflicts. If you cannot secure a bus, ask for volunteer drivers (resolving school or district insurance issues beforehand).
- Use public transportation if available.

Telephones/faxes
- Talk to administrators and office workers about your project, assuring them that students are adequately trained to use the phone appropriately.
- Use a sign-up sheet for access to existing phones.
- It may make sense to install a class phone, using funds from the school district, special grant funds or gifts from local businesses.
- If older students have cellular phones, request permission to use their phones for the project on certain days, reimbursing them for calls.

"Whether we recognize it or not, we are capable of an impact that is huge."

— *Tenth-grade student, Oxford Hills High School, South Paris, Maine*

Evaluate the Project's Impact

In addition to implementing a solution, students need to evaluate the impact and effectiveness of their project—from their own and the community's perspective. This process occurs during their service-learning process—in the form of reflection—and again once their project is complete. Thoroughly evaluating a project's impact helps students think critically about what they have learned, what they have contributed to their community, and what they will carry with them as they move forward. Through the process of evaluation, students often gain a broader perspective on what they have accomplished, and a deep sense of satisfaction at making a difference.

As their project winds down, students should revisit their original project description and determine if they've had a positive impact on the problem they defined. If students gathered baseline data earlier in their project, they can analyze how that compares to more recent findings--looking at both qualitative and quantitative measures of change. Pre- and post-surveys, interviews, and observations are just a few ways for students to evaluate the impacts they have made. Whatever mode students use, they should always include their community partners in this process.

To gain a more formal and objective picture of the project's impact, students may devise and distribute a survey to people affected by the project.

▶ How did the project benefit the community?

▶ Do those affected by the project value the outcome? How and why?

▶ What could have been done differently?

▶ Did the project meet the community's standard for quality work? Why or why not?

(The Community Partner Survey Form, in the Appendix on pages 118-119, may serve as a possible survey tool.)

Election Project: Evaluate the Project's Impact

Reflection

It was important to include many perspectives in evaluating the project's impact on the problem and its overall success.

▶ Students conducted a post-election survey of those who attended the community center "Get out the Vote" party. They asked if the party made any difference in their voting. They compared these results with the pre-survey results they had collected earlier.

▶ Students debriefed with the Town Clerk after the election. They reviewed their data to see if they had met their goal of increasing voter turnout by 10 percent.

▶ Students wrote in their journals about the impact the project had on themselves and others and why or why not the project was successful.

Chapter 7:
Take Service-Learning
to the Next Level

Case Study: Commit to Service-Learning

Reflect on Your Service-Learning Practice

> Tool: KIDS Checklist for a Successful Service-
> Learning Project

Progress to New Projects

> Sidebar: When to Continue an Existing Project

Find Allies and Recruit Others

> Tool: Make the Case for Service-Learning

> Sidebar: Advocate for Service-Learning

Integrate Service-Learning into School Systems

> Tool: Questions for Your Service-Learning Leadership
> Team

> Tool: Vision and Goals for Systemic Integration of
> Service-Learning

Look to the Future

"I've really come to be a true believer in the value of service-learning. It is the single biggest change we've made in our curriculum that has made the most difference for our kids. In service-learning, students are all working together to solve common problems. We seldom do that in public education, and it's a powerful thing."

— *Rob Liebow, superintendent, Mount Desert Island Regional School System, Maine*

Case Study: Commit to Service-Learning

Service-learning is now an integral part of the Mount Desert Island Regional School System's STARS framework which fosters in students Service, leadership and citizenship; Technology readiness; Academic development; Resiliency, health and wellness; and Social and character development. Working closely with KIDS Consortium since 2003, MDIRSS has adopted a rigorous, student-directed model of service-learning. What began in 2003 with 5 service-learning projects involving 60 students has grown into 50 projects engaging 600 students (as of 2010). Through collaborative efforts overseen by a local leadership team, the school system has created policies and dedicated the necessary funding to sustain and expand service-learning opportunities.

MDIRSS Assistant Superintendent Joanne Harriman receives service-learning sustainability award.

As service-learning began taking hold in the school system, MDIRSS committed to ensuring that students would have service-learning experiences through all grades and multiple content areas. All 8th graders, for example, now participate in Project Citizen, learning public policy through work on a service-learning project. Ninth-graders all take a year-long Global Literacies class that culminates in student-led service-learning projects.

The service-learning projects address both local concerns (such as cultivating a threatened fish species or monitoring local water quality) and universal challenges (such as reducing energy consumption, waste generation, and underage drinking). Through these initiatives, MDIRSS superintendent Rob Liebow notes, "community members have come to see students in a different light." That positive impression of the students and schools has helped the school system at budget time.

Service-learning on Mount Desert Island is advanced by a local leadership team that is comprised of enthusiastic teachers, students and community members, the district's Assistant Superintendent (who oversees curriculum development), and designated "building representatives"—teachers who are service-learning contacts and coaches for peers in their schools. Building representatives and the district service-learning coordinator are available to help teachers plan projects and work through issues that arise. The team plans and schedules varied and continuous professional development opportunities for teachers; promotes greater understanding of service-learning; and helps the district incorporate service-learning into its annual plans and actions.

Perseverance is key to the school system's success, and the service-learning team works continually to get more people understanding and implementing high-quality service-learning. At MDIRSS, teachers have grown into their roles as service-learning leaders over a number of years, evolving from early pioneers to experienced practitioners and then coaches supporting their peers. "This kind of change takes time," says MDIRSS Assistant Superintendent Joanne Harriman. "It's like cultivating a garden, where you need to invest effort season after season."

Reflect on Your Service-Learning Practice

As your service-learning project winds down, take time to reflect on how the project went and what areas could be improved in future projects.

▶ One tool for a structured assessment is the KIDS Checklist for a Successful Service-Learning Project (below and in the Appendix on page 120)—which helps you gauge how your project aligns with the three KIDS principles: academic integrity, apprentice citizenship and student ownership.

▶ Another reflection strategy is to ask students for feedback on the service-learning process.

▶ To evaluate how well your project met National K-12 Standards for Quality Service-Learning Practice, refer to Assessing Your Service-Learning Practice in the Appendix on pages 121-122.

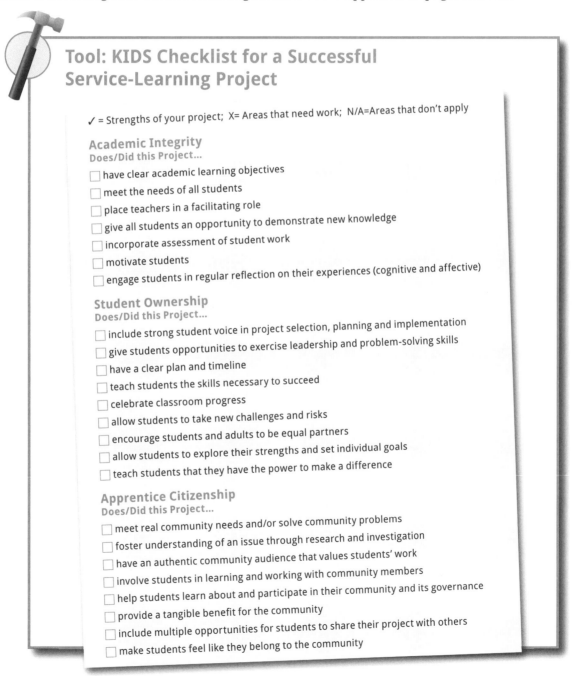

Tool: KIDS Checklist for a Successful Service-Learning Project

✓ = Strengths of your project; X= Areas that need work; N/A=Areas that don't apply

Academic Integrity
Does/Did this Project...
☐ have clear academic learning objectives
☐ meet the needs of all students
☐ place teachers in a facilitating role
☐ give all students an opportunity to demonstrate new knowledge
☐ incorporate assessment of student work
☐ motivate students
☐ engage students in regular reflection on their experiences (cognitive and affective)

Student Ownership
Does/Did this Project...
☐ include strong student voice in project selection, planning and implementation
☐ give students opportunities to exercise leadership and problem-solving skills
☐ have a clear plan and timeline
☐ teach students the skills necessary to succeed
☐ celebrate classroom progress
☐ allow students to take new challenges and risks
☐ encourage students and adults to be equal partners
☐ allow students to explore their strengths and set individual goals
☐ teach students that they have the power to make a difference

Apprentice Citizenship
Does/Did this Project...
☐ meet real community needs and/or solve community problems
☐ foster understanding of an issue through research and investigation
☐ have an authentic community audience that values students' work
☐ involve students in learning and working with community members
☐ help students learn about and participate in their community and its governance
☐ provide a tangible benefit for the community
☐ include multiple opportunities for students to share their project with others
☐ make students feel like they belong to the community

As you anticipate next steps, you may be wondering how you will grow your practice of service-learning. What do you need (in the way of networking, professional development, and mentoring) to keep learning and growing? The support you need may depend on whether you've completed one or two projects and want to build your skills or whether you're a more experienced practitioner seeking to expand or improve your practice.

Gaining Experience: Planning and Implementing Projects

Teachers who have done a project or two but feel a need to strengthen their practice can seek out trainings that focus on aspects of service-learning such as:

▶ strategies to support youth voice and diverse learning styles in project planning and implementation;

▶ techniques for creating a collaborative classroom environment;

▶ approaches to building partnerships and using school and community resources;

▶ the role of reflection in supporting service-learning;

▶ resources available locally and nationally to support service-learning;

▶ current research on service-learning and its impacts on students, teachers, and communities; and

▶ curriculum planning, instruction, and assessment.

Reflective Practice: Improving the Service-Learning Experience

Experienced practitioners of service-learning still can benefit from skill development, learning more about the National K-12 Standards for Quality Service-Learning Practice (see www.nylc.org) and doing self-assessments to identify strengths and areas for improvement. Feedback from peers and small-group reflection can help determine ways to achieve and sustain best practices in the context of a school and district. To gain more support in these areas, teachers can talk further with their local service-learning coordinator or with a curriculum director or building administrator in their district. Information on relevant state and national trainings and conferences is also available through KIDS Consortium.

Progress to New Projects

By completing a service-learning project, you've improved the lives of your students and community in far-reaching ways, ones that may be measured for years to come. You've followed the KIDS Framework (page 14), reaching the end of one trail. Now, you must decide which path to venture down next year. Most teachers choose one of three options:

▶ Start with a Different Entry Point than previous year
(New Topic/Problems and Solution/ Approaches)

▶ Start with the Same Entry Point as previous year – but students work on new solutions
(Same Topic/Problem- new approach to addressing it)

▶ Start with the Same Entry Point as previous year and students continue with the same solution
(Same Topic/Problem and similar approach to addressing it)

"I was able to write proposals, and collaborate with people in my class to make educated decisions about how to communicate our proposal to others. With other students, I compiled materials for a Master Plan to show anyone who would listen to us. I learned how to research and document facts, and how to organize my random thoughts on paper...I finally found something that I could do to make me feel good inside and make a difference in my own world."

— *Greg Lavertu, former student at Edward Little High School, Auburn, Maine*

There may be good reasons to start with an entirely new Entry Point each year: you may have great curricular flexibility and not be bound by content; there might be a current issue that fits perfectly with your curriculum; or you may have met a community partner with a pressing need that meshes well with your curriculum. Teachers often find it easier, though, to start with a similar entry point as past years that fits into their curriculum and allows students to investigate and come up with their own solutions. Students may come up with solutions similar to previous years, but it's important to take them through the whole KIDS Framework (page 14) and not begin with a predetermined solution. The last option (Same Entry Point and Same Solution) should be considered only in cases where the original service-learning project was too ambitious to complete fully in a single school year or requires ongoing stewardship (see sidebar on When to Continue an Existing Project).

When to Continue an Existing Project

In some cases, you may need to invite a new class to continue work on a project already started. Projects like a school garden or water-quality monitoring often require multiple years of student involvement to succeed. While a new class may need to continue certain facets of a project, it helps if students can take ownership of some new dimension. If students are not enthusiastic about a project, consider retiring it for a year (with the option of returning to it with a subsequent class). Research indicates that service-learning projects succeed best when students take full ownership, so make time for your new class to learn about the problem/need and agree on a solution (rather than assuming they'll adopt the previous group's solution).

In the case of a water-quality monitoring project, for example, a new class might decide to supplement basic data-gathering with a community outreach effort, informing residents about ways to minimize nonpoint source pollution. A class taking responsibility for a school garden might forge a new partnership with a homeless shelter, planning crops that will meet the needs of their residents. Or they might decide to work on a "garden vegetable" cookbook or a seed sale that encourages school families to grow kitchen gardens. While inheriting some basic project responsibilities from a previous class, the new class can approach the identified problem/need and solution with fresh eyes and create a project that reflects their interests and perspectives.

The "Discover Needs and Problems" section in Chapter 4 (see page 50) offers specific ideas for how best to engage students in projects. If students select a project that will extend beyond the school year, it's important to:

▶ set reasonable goals for what students can accomplish in the time allotted;

▶ see if the project is connected to other content areas or classes so that more students can become involved;

▶ periodically celebrate their achievement;

▶ carefully document their vision for the project (through maps, charts, written materials, etc.—see Documenting the Project on page 75); and

▶ brainstorm how students might "pass the torch" to others.

Teachers and students who take over an existing project will want to:

▶ have students from the previous year (and potentially community partners and teachers) brief them on the project's history and current status;

▶ review documentation compiled to date; and

▶ brainstorm ideas for how the project might grow and transform (offering new students more ownership of the project).

Find Allies and Recruit Others

Service-learning tends to be easier, more fun and more influential when teams of teachers adopt it. To generate in-building support for service-learning, you can chat informally with colleagues about your experiences and share the resources you've found most helpful. On KIDS Consortium surveys, teachers have cited the following factors as their biggest draws to service-learning:

▶ wanting to overcome students' lack of engagement in learning;

▶ frustration at not reaching kids with different "intelligences" and learning styles; and

▶ a sense that past teaching approaches weren't helping students become effective and engaged citizens.

Teachers intrigued by the potential of service-learning sometimes feel unsure of how to begin, and what pitfalls they might encounter. Hearing about your experience and reading about other service-learning case studies (in this guide and at www.kidsconsortium.org) may dispel those concerns.

You can further expand your network of allies and recruit others through the following means:

▶ Share the benefits and results of service-learning projects with the school and the larger community—having students tell their story through exhibits, presentations and written summaries (e.g., in the school newsletter, local newspaper and appropriate social media).

▶ Invite other classes (from other grade levels or schools) to participate in aspects of the service-learning project. If you teach on a team, consider developing an integrated unit that incorporates service-learning into two or more content areas—an initiative that fosters teacher collaboration, engages more students in service-learning, and often creates larger time blocks in which students can accomplish their projects.

Students present their project to teachers and administrators.

▶ Invite students and teachers to present at faculty/curriculum meetings, demonstrating how service-learning fosters best practices in instruction and assessment.

▶ Ask your school district to offer summer curriculum funds and mini-grants to help teachers launch new service-learning projects.

▶ Request that the district provide in-service programs on service-learning and encourage school administrators to attend. Consult KIDS Consortium for more information on customized offerings and for appropriate contacts within each state.

Tool: Make the Case for Service-Learning

For service-learning to succeed in your school, you may need to convince others to integrate service-learning into the curriculum. With limited time to make this case, it helps to be well prepared. Here are some talking points you may wish to incorporate.

For Administrators and School Board Members:

▶ Research studies (see http://www.nylc.org/standards-effective-service-learning-practice) confirm that service-learning increases academic achievement (as measured by grades and standardized test scores); reduces attendance problems; and fosters greater civic involvement (among participating students and their families).

▶ Service-learning improves the culture and climate of the school by fostering greater student responsibility and cooperation.

▶ Service-learning develops critical thinking skills and problem-solving by engaging students in meaningful, real-world challenges that build their content knowledge, creativity and confidence. Students gain 21st century skills (such as collaboration and communication) that improve their performance—not just in school—but in life.

▶ Service-learning builds valuable and enduring bridges with the community, fostering good relations that extend well beyond the students' school careers. Students better understand the community's needs and challenges, and gain a sense of citizenship and civic commitment. Community members get new insights into how schools enhance their community and may see students (and school budgets) in a more positive light.

For Teachers:

▶ Service-learning rejuvenates teachers, renewing their enthusiasm and sense of purpose. It revitalizes content areas that may have become rote. It helps make the curriculum relevant to students, and fosters a constructive classroom climate.

▶ Service-learning fosters collaboration and greater responsibility among students, engaging both high-performing students and those who struggle with traditional modes of teaching. The experiential nature of service-learning projects draws on multiple intelligences and can help students find new strengths, gain confidence, and emerge as leaders.

▶ Students work collaboratively to define and address the identified problem, shaping solutions themselves rather than being told "the right answer." They learn first-hand about the importance of education and community participation—often gaining some of the most memorable learning experiences they've ever had.

Students thank community members at the end of the school year.

Advocate for Service-Learning

When you're making the case for service-learning before school boards and other decision-makers, it can help to have your remarks clearly outlined in advance. Create a succinct script (keeping your remarks to 5 minutes) that communicates the benefits service-learning affords students, teachers and communities. Strive to be clear and convincing. Here's a sample script that demonstrates how one teacher, Patricia Nilan from Massachusetts, summarized the benefits of service-learning to administrators in her district.

Good Afternoon. For those who don't know me, my name is Trish Nilan. As a teacher, I'm convinced that service-learning will benefit our students, school, community, and you. Since becoming involved in service-learning projects, I have directly seen their positive impact on our students. I would like to share some of what I have observed.

Service-learning is more than just community service work: it's a teaching strategy that combines our curriculum with community problems and needs. Students use existing and new content knowledge to effectively address community problems, "learning while doing." This process helps them develop the skills they need to be effective citizens and successful in all facets of their lives.

Research shows that service-learning enhances academic achievement, measured by both grades and standardized test scores. It does this by making learning relevant, increasing motivation (and improving student attendance) and engaging students at all levels (including students "at risk"). Students gain confidence in themselves and become more engaged in their community. Those who participate in service-learning projects are more likely to become active citizens, volunteers, and voters. They acquire skills such as collaboration, communication and problem-solving that will benefit them throughout life.

I have mentioned many benefits for the student, but what about for us teachers? I have found that service-learning helps me look at teaching through different eyes. It's exciting to see the students get so involved, and we all feel a sense of accomplishment at being able to help the community. There is now a real purpose to my teaching: I am teaching the "whole" student, and preparing our future adults to make informed decisions.

Finally, there is a benefit for our community, locally and globally. We are directly helping with issues, and indirectly helping by cultivating effective citizens.

Given the many benefits from service-learning, I hope you will join me in helping make this a greater part of our school and community. Thank you.

Integrate Service-Learning into School Systems

As service-learning becomes more established within a school or district, proponents often shift from a classroom orientation to a systemic one, working strategically to unite people and resources and forge an integrated and ongoing commitment to service-learning.

Service-learning succeeds best when teachers join forces and work collaboratively with school administrators, district curriculum coordinators, community members and others. As more teachers and students participate in service-learning, you may want to create a "leadership team" that works to systematically integrate service-learning. The team's first task is to determine the scale of its work.

▶ Is your team working to integrate service-learning throughout the building or the entire district?

▶ Are there others who need to be part of the decision-making process?

▶ Does your school or district have initiatives underway that service-learning could support (e.g., health and wellness, literacy, drop-out prevention, STEM, and technology integration)?

The questions outlined in the tool Questions for Your Service-Learning Leadership Team (below) may help guide these initial conversations.

Tool: Questions for Your Service-Learning Leadership Team

▶ How does service-learning fit as a strategy to implement the school's or district's visions and goals?

▶ How does service-learning support or enhance educational reform initiatives already underway?

▶ How will service-learning projects connect with standards, curriculum and the local assessment plan?

▶ Will the administration support professional development and planning time for teachers?

▶ Which community officials and organizations are most apt to be interested in a partnership with students?

▶ What level of parent and community involvement will be required?

▶ What resources will be needed and which are available now?

▶ How might service-learning affect other budgets and priorities in the coming year and beyond?

In its consulting work with schools and school districts, KIDS Consortium has found that leadership teams succeed best when they work to integrate service-learning into the strategic planning process that already directs actions and funding priorities. To help organize this approach, it may be useful to create a vision and goals specific to service-learning within these four areas (see the tool Vision and Goals for Systematic Integration of Service-Learning (page 90):

▶ Leadership;

▶ Curriculum, Instruction and Assessment;

▶ Professional Development; and

▶ School/Community Partnerships.

Having a clear vision for the future will make it easier for your service-learning leadership team to identify concrete implementation strategies and advocate to include those in the school's or district's broader planning documents. As you work to integrate service-learning in this way, you can get practical and moral support from many sources—including KIDS Consortium, other school districts with service-learning experience, and your state department of education and/or service commission.

Tool: Vision and Goals for Systemic Integration of Service-Learning

The following sample vision and goal statements evolved from work KIDS Consortium has done with school districts. These statements incorporate key ideas to help embed service-learning in a school's or district's policy, practice and culture. (KIDS Consortium has many examples of specific strategies that school districts have used to implement their vision and goals.)

Leadership

Sample vision: A multi-faceted leadership effort continually advocates for, supports and evaluates service-learning practice to ensure its vibrancy and prosperity. Strategic plans and initiatives have explicit policies and practices that encourage and support service-learning.

Sample Goals:

▶ A leadership team, which includes a service-learning coordinator, works to establish and sustain structures and supports for service-learning.

▶ Policies and practices are in place to advocate for, support and evaluate service-learning.

Curriculum, Instruction and Assessment

Sample Vision: All students have multiple opportunities to implement high-quality service-learning projects that develop strong academic knowledge, social skills and civic attitudes. Projects are embedded in, but not limited to, designated grade-level curriculum, instruction and assessment requirements.

Sample Goals:

▶ Service-learning is integrated into the curriculum and aligned with national and state standards and the district's vision. At least one service-learning experience occurs in each grade span (lower elementary, upper elementary, middle and high) and in other learning opportunities.

▶ High-quality instruction occurs in all service-learning projects.

▶ Assessment demonstrates that service-learning is an effective strategy through which students master developmentally appropriate academic knowledge, social skills and civic attitudes.

Professional Development

Sample vision: All staff and relevant community members can participate in high-quality professional development experiences focused on service-learning. They have opportunities to understand service-learning; develop tools and strategies to implement projects; and reflect with others on their service-learning experience.

Sample Goals:

▶ All school staff (including teachers, after-school providers, extra-curricular advisors, ed techs, cafeteria staff, bus drivers, office staff, and administrators), community members/organizations, and students thoroughly understand service-learning and its benefits.

▶ School staff and community partners involved in service-learning have the knowledge, skills and support needed to facilitate high-quality experiences with students.

School/Community Partnerships

Sample vision: Both schools and communities use service-learning to strengthen K-12 education and constructively address community needs. School/community partnerships are nurtured and sustained over time.

Sample Goals:

▶ Community members and/or organizations seek student involvement in solving problems and needs.

▶ School staff works with appropriate community partners (organizations or individuals with expertise to share) on opportunities for partnerships that address authentic problems/needs.

▶ Both the school and community organizations have structures and processes in place to continually develop and sustain constructive service-learning partnerships.

Look to the Future

As you work to integrate service-learning into your classroom and district, you'll need to be patient and persistent, recognizing that substantive changes take time. Stay inspired by connecting with others in your school and community who share your commitment to engage students in meaningful service-learning. Take opportunities to network with service-learning practitioners from around the country at workshops, conferences and other gatherings. Continue building your skills and sharing your service-learning experiences with others. And, most important of all, keep offering your students learning opportunities that will enrich them in school and in life.

Appendix

Core Principles for the KIDS As Planners Model of Service-Learning

Academic Integrity

Integrated: Integral part of academic program

All Learners: Meets needs of all students

Facilitated: Teachers play important facilitation role

Learning and Assessment: Students apply and demonstrate new knowledge and critical skills

Relevant: School is relevant and students are motivated to learn

Student Ownership

Student-driven: Students select, plan and implement projects

Adventure: Projects involve challenge and risk-taking

Partnerships: Students and adults are equal partners

Self-awareness: Students explore their strengths to set goals and solve problems

Students Matter: Students learn they have the power to make a difference

Apprentice Citizenship

Belonging: Students feel as though they belong to a community

Authenticity: Students' work is valued because it meets real community needs

Community Expertise: Students learn with and from community members

Civic Awareness: Students become effective citizens

KIDS Framework Planning Sheet

Curriculum Instruction and Assessment

Goal: connect the service-learning project directly to curriculum, instruction and assessment

Celebration

Goal: build ongoing enthusiasm for the project and recognize accomplishments

Public Relations

Goal: make sure the public is aware of the project

Collaborative Environment

Goal: create effective teamwork among class members

Reflection

Goal: make connections between the project and the learnings of the students

Evaluate the Impacts

Goal: evaluate the impacts of the project

Implement the Plan

Goal: put a plan into action and complete the project

Plan the Project

Goal: create an action plan for the project

Decide on a Project

Goal: evaluate solutions and select a project

Research Solutions

Goal: identify and research possible solutions

Investigate Problems

Goal: investigate cause and effect of the identified problems

Discover Needs/ Problems

Goal: identify relevant and interesting needs/problems

Define Service-Learning

Goal: understand service-learning

Sample KIDS Project Ideas

The following list summarizes just a few of the many creative KIDS projects that have been successfully completed. For a more extensive compilation organized by age range and subject, please visit http://www.kidsconsortium.org.

▶ After researching the impact of non-point source pollution on their local bay, middle school students created brochures, informational packets, public service announcements and a website featuring ways to reduce pollution.

▶ During a trip to the waste management center, 4th grade students learned about mercury thermometer collection. After researching the harmful effects of mercury pollution, they worked with the center to inform residents about the issue and to host a Thermometer Exchange Day.

▶ Worried about heavy traffic near their school, elementary students collected data and presented their findings to the local police department and town council. Their actions resulted in the installation of a much-needed traffic light.

▶ While completing a community mapping project to identify resources for children, alternative education students discovered that many lacked bicycles. Working with the school social worker and local bike shop, students refurbished and distributed bicycles to children who needed them.

▶ After learning that emergency responders lose critical time when called to a fire or accident because of possible hazards and lack of access ways, 10th graders worked with the fire chief and town manager to survey residents of a particular neighborhood. Using a Geographic Information System (GIS) to map potential hazards, students created a prototype map of the neighborhood and presented it to the Town Council and local firefighters.

▶ When 5th graders in a health class learned that childhood obesity is a growing problem in their state and across the country, they decided to plan the school's annual fun run. Students worked with numerous community partners, researched health publications, and wrote letters to community members inviting them to participate.

▶ Inspired by Ron Suskind's A Hope in the Unseen, high school students in their social studies class decided to raise community awareness about hunger. Students hosted an Oxfam Hunger Banquet and asked for donations at the door, giving the collected money to a local food bank. Using information from their research, they presented information on local and global hunger to all the Banquet participants.

▶ During a class field trip to their state capitol, 2nd graders discovered there was no tourist information specifically for children. Working with the Capitol Region Visitor Center and local libraries, students created a Kid's Guide to their city. The students designed the cover, wrote the content, drew illustrations, and took their work to a local print shop that copied and bound the guide.

▶ During their visit to a nearby animal shelter, students got a first-hand look at the hardships shelter animals face and learned from staff about animal mistreatment and proper care of pets. After researching Animal Rescue League materials, the students decided to educate others in their school by working with the technology teacher to develop several YouTube videos directed toward pre-K through 5th graders.

Create a Project Overview Circle

Topic(s)/Problem(s)
Will students explore multiple topics, a single topic, or a single problem? List topic(s)/problems that students will explore.

Topic:

Possible problems:

Community Partners
Who benefits from the service?

What experts can help with the project?

Student Ownership
How will students discover the need?

What decisions will they make along the way to solve the problem?

Academic Integrity
How does this project connect with the curriculum?

Create a Project Learning Web

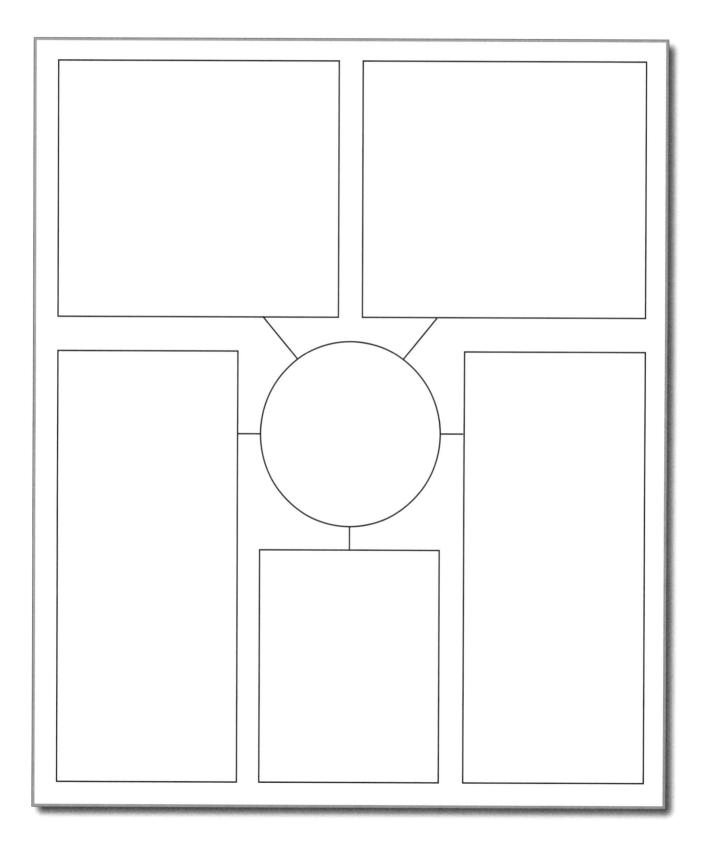

Planning Backwards

Learning Objective	Assessing Prior Knowledge	Instructional Activities	Assessment Tasks	Assessment Tools
What are the learning objectives? (i.e., your state/local standards)	How will you assess prior student knowledge of these objectives?	What instructional activities (e.g., mini-lessons, practice debates) will you use to teach objectives, including opportunities for students to practice their new knowledge and skills?	What are the tasks (i.e., products and performances) by which students will demonstrate achievement of these objectives?	What assessment tool (e.g., rubric, product descriptor) will you use to provide feedback to students?

Use "The Being" to Develop Norms

This exercise provides a way for elementary school students to visualize those behaviors that they want to include in their group and those they prefer to exclude.

1. Place on the floor a bed sheet or scroll of butcher paper that is longer and wider than a student.

2. Ask a student to lie down on it, face up.

3. Invite one or two other students to trace an outline of the prone student with a marker. The student's outline then becomes a representation of the body or "being" of the group.

4. Both students and teachers can brainstorm what behaviors make a group work well together, using one- or two-word descriptions and recording them on a separate paper or chalkboard.

5. Once the list is complete, have group members distill 6-7 key attributes that they write within the body in one color.

6. Return to brainstorming and generate a list of elements that could detract from the positive dynamics. Select 6-7 factors that might disrupt the group process; scatter those outside the body in a different color.

7. Finally, have group members come up with a name for their "being" and label that over the body.

If you choose to post the "being" on a classroom wall, students can make check marks by certain attributes or detractors when they witness them in action. The "being" can also be a helpful reminder when the group discusses progress, noting what's working and what's not.

— adapted from Adventure in the Classroom *by Mary Henton and* Project Adventure. *Dubuque, IA: Kendall-Hunt,*

Ice Breakers

Human Scrabble
Give everyone a 5x7 card that has a letter on it and about a minute to join with others to form words as quickly as possible. Depending on the group size, words must be at least 3 letters. Nonsense words are permitted but the group must create a definition for them. Have group mix several times. Consider suggesting categories to which words must relate.

Mapping Game
Indicate to group where North/South/East and West is. Ask group members to place themselves on this imaginary map according to criteria such as where they were born; where they have traveled recently; the farthest point they have traveled from home or their dream vacation destination. Encourage sharing of the locations they chose.

Name Race
In a circle, have group members say their names consecutively as fast as possible. Starting (counterclockwise) towards the right is Team A. Repeat several times to get the best time (world's record) for Team A. Try this same challenge with Team B (going (clockwise to the left of the leader). Pit Team A against Team B.

Face Off
Divide group into partners and create with them 3 facial expressions-gestures-noises. Have the partners stand back-to-back. On the count of three, partners turn and "face off" with one of the three expressions—perhaps the same one as their partner. Repeat several times, trying to match expressions.

Heads/Tails Tag
Demonstrate gestures for Heads (hand on head) and Tails (hand on rear end). Each group member determines which they are at start of game. Those who are Heads try to tag Tails and vice versa. If a Head tags a Tail, the Tail becomes a Head. Play until all players become the same thing. Keep boundaries small.

Puzle Activity
Create blank puzzle pieces out of cardboard. Mark the back so you know which side is the front. Ask group members to draw things that are important to them in their world. Give about 10 min. to draw. Have group members share. After everyone has shared, put the puzzle together.

Fill Me In
Have group members get in a circle. A leader points to someone across the circle, says their name, and then moves into their place. That person repeats this action and the action continues until the last group member points to the first person again. You can repeat the game in the same order to establish a speed record.

Name Mingle
Start with a Name Toss or some Name Game. Get in a circle and make sure you know the names of the people on your immediate left/right. Have group members mingle with their Bumpers Up (hands up) first with eyes opened then closed. Ask them to return to the original circle configuration with eyes closed (talking is permissible).

Ice Breakers (cont.)

Zip/Zap/Zooey

Start in a circle. The leader, in the middle, points at someone and says ZIP. That person ducks as fast a possible and the two on either side of him/her point at each other and say ZAP. The person who Zaps the other person first is "Safe;" the slower Zapper goes into the middle to replace the leader. Game continues like this.

2nd level

Leader points at someone and instead of Zip-says Zooey. The "Zooeyed" person must remain standing. If s/he ducks, s/he comes in the middle.

3rd level

Every time someone is "Zapped," have them sit down where they are. They have been eliminated for this round. Game continues until only a few remain.

Left/Right Name Juggle

With group members in a circle, pass a ball to the right and say that person's name (and remember it). Pass the ball around the circle several times in this mode. Then mix up the order of the circle. Now toss the ball to the person who was on your right previously, and ask others to do the same. When the group has done this once or twice, add in more balls.

100 Seconds

Ask group members to pair up with a person they don't usually work with and take 100 seconds to find out three interesting things they have in common (ones not apparent by looking at them). When the 100 seconds are up, ask them to share in pairs.

Snowball Activity

Group members write on a piece of paper three things about themselves. Then they crumple the paper up into a 'snowball' and have a one-minute snowball fight. At the end of the minute, each person grabs the closest snowball and tries to find the person who wrote it. They then introduce that person to the group, sharing the three facts.

Venn Diagram

Form pairs and hand each pair a blank Venn Diagram form (two intersecting circles). Each person in the pair writes his/her name at the top of one circle and then tries to list 3-5 things in the overlapping portion that they have in common. Each can then list 3-5 unique things in their part of their circle. Pairs can share findings with the group.

A Tangled Web

Gather group members in a circle. With a large ball of yarn, share your name and something about yourself and then roll the ball of yarn to a group member while holding the end of the yarn. That person says his/her name and something additional and then rolls the yarn to somebody else, holding on to a strand. Soon students have created a giant web and can see how essential group participation is to teamwork (and what happens if one person drops the yarn).

Meet and Greet

Ask group members to circulate and meet new people, doing three things:
shake hand; state names and tell three interesting facts about themselves.

Have them continue doing this with new people for 5-10 minutes, greeting as many people as possible. Then ask participants to go back, find the people they met., and try to remember their name and the three things they mentioned.

Different Preferences for Group Work

Similar to the Myers-Briggs Personality Inventory, this exercise uses a set of preferences which relate not to individual but to group behaviors, helping to understand how preferences affect group work.

1. Set up signs—Structure, Meaning, Action, Caring—on each of four walls. Include by each sign a writing utensil and paper with 5 questions at each corner (see those listed at the end of this activity).

2. Explain the following to the group:
When people work together in groups, individuals often have a preference for how common work is undertaken. There are four common preferences:

▶ **Structure:** these individuals want a structure apparent so that everyone knows the "rules of the game"— being clear about how and by whom decisions are made, the form of meetings, the way in which visions will be developed, and the progression of work. Without a structure in place, they may feel things are useless or disorganized.

▶ **Meaning:** these individuals need a common understanding of the meaning and vision for the work at hand (without that, they feel, nothing else can be clear). From meaning comes clarity about what kind of structure is appropriate and what kind of action will reflect the meaning.

▶ **Action:** Action is the core preference for some, who just want to DO IT (not talking endlessly) and refine things as needed once undertaken. For them, structure and meaning emerge from action.

▶ **Caring:** these individuals want to understand the strengths and contributions that each person can make and establish a process with clear group norms to foster cohesiveness, minimize conflict and solve problems.

3. Invite students to go to the corner that represents their common preference for group work. While no individual has only one preference, each person can choose their dominant preference.

4. Have the students in each corner answer the questions at the end of this activity and then report back to the whole group. Notice the kinds of questions/statements each corner uses:

▶ Caring folks ask "How is everyone feeling about this? Do we need a break?"

▶ Structure folks ask "When, how, who says, how long, what time?

▶ Action folks say "Enough talk, just DO IT!"

▶ Meaning folks ask "Why are we doing this? What is the purpose here? Does this matter?"

5. Invite the group to consider the meaning of this distribution among the corners. If it's lopsided, what might happen? For example, a group with mainly Meaning, a few Action and Caring people and no Structure people might tend to talk far too much, frustrating the Action people. They might need to develop a workable structure since no one naturally assumed that role. If any students remain in the center, you can point out two possible consequences of that position: those individuals can see all preferences and help facilitate a balance, or they may jump all over the place without being able to decide what's important.

Encourage the group to consider the following questions: What is the best combination for a group to have? Does it matter? How can you avoid being driven crazy by another preference? Discuss how awareness of different preferences can help promote understanding of each other's strengths and diffuse tensions. For example, Meaning and Action group members can grow frustrated if they lose sight of what the other perspective brings to the process.

Questions for Each Group:
Decide which of the four Preferences most closely describes your personal style when doing group work. Then spend 15 minutes answering the following questions as a group.

1. What are the strengths of your style? (4 adjectives)

2. What are the limitations of your style? (4 adjectives)

3. What style do you find most difficult to work with and why?

4. What do people from the other "directions" or styles need to know about you so you can work together effectively?

5. What do you value about the other three styles?

Team Communication Check-In

Circle the most accurate number for each statement.

1=Awful	2=Fair	3=Good	4=Great

A. We listened to each other's ideas.

1   2   3   4

B. Everyone got a chance to participate.

1   2   3   4

C. We stayed on task.

1   2   3   4

D. We encouraged each other.

1   2   3   4

E. We made decisions as a team.

1   2   3   4

Effective Citizen Brainstorm

In the course of completing service-learning projects, it can be helpful for students to reflect on the meaning of engaged citizenship—creating for themselves a list of the knowledge/skills, attitudes/beliefs and behaviors/ actions of an active and effective participant in our democracy.

Break the class into three groups and explain that each group will be responsible for one of the three categories (knowledge/skills, attitudes/beliefs, and behaviors/actions). Give each group 10-15 minutes to develop ideas in its category and come up with a list of qualities, using the brainstorming guidance on page 53.

There are several ways that groups can report back results:

1. Post their list on the wall and invite class members to add input and star the items they feel are most important. When this is complete, ask the original group to read the top responses.

2. Ask each group to read their list. Then ask the rest of the class to state which they feel are the most important and suggest new items for the list.

3. Have each group brainstorm on a body part: knowledge/ skills-Head Neck, attitudes/beliefs - Torso and behaviors/ actions-Limbs. As groups report out, put together the effective citizen with all of its parts.

In reflecting and debriefing on the brainstorming sessions, invite class members to discuss the following questions: How did this activity enhance your understanding of effective citizenship? How might this activity work with students or other groups?

Following the activity, you may choose to post the lists students created on the classroom wall, adding items throughout the year.

Investigate the Problem

KWL *Know • Want • Learn*

What do we KNOW about our problem?	What do we WANT or need to know about our problem? (i.e., cause, effect, and history or problem)	How will we LEARN what we want/need?

Field Research

Finding Primary Materials

Students may learn of documents or data in the community that can help expand their understanding of the problem they've defined. They may need to make site visits to read through these materials, whether they are historical reports, maps or databases. Students can use phone interviews to identify where the most relevant information is located, and then set up appointments to do further research on-site. It may be helpful to discuss plans and share information (via phone, e-mail or site visits) with students and teachers from other schools that have done similar projects.

Locating Secondary Information

Using the Internet, library reference departments, and bookstores, students may identify specialized publications and sites related to the problem they have identified. Students may also discover audio-visual resources (videos, television/radio documentaries and programs, podcasts) that provide more context for the problem they're exploring. Ask a librarian at your school or a local library to teach your students how to effectively navigate these resources.

Inviting Speakers to Class

Speakers from the community can visit the classroom to share their perspectives on issues students have identified. If your school district has a volunteer coordinator, seek their help identifying appropriate community experts and organizations. In arranging for these visits, students should provide as much information as possible about the subject, audience and any honorarium or travel stipend that might be available. Once a speaker has committed to come, students should follow up with a letter reiterating the date, time and location (providing directions, a map and information on where to park and enter the school building), and giving additional background information on the school/class project— including a list of questions they would like to discuss. Have students greet speakers upon their arrival, and arrange for their meals and lodging (if necessary). Following the visit, students should write thank-you letters expressing what they learned from the talk.

Conducting Interviews and Focus Groups

Students may choose to interview community members, either by phone, in person, or via email. Before making any calls, students should review proper phoning etiquette (see Interview Forms on pages 108 and 109). Have students draft notes on what they will ask, and keep a phone log recording with whom they spoke, their title, address and phone extension, and the information provided. Students may need to contact people repeatedly if calls are not returned: they can be persistent as long as they're polite. At the beginning of their calls, students should state their name, grade and school.

For in-person interviews, have students prepare questions in advance and call to set up an appointment (see Interview Forms on pages 108 and 109). Students can practice asking questions of each other initially, getting coached on speaking clearly and slowly. Role plays (that include both "easy" and "challenging" interviewees) offer an enjoyable way for students to gain skills and confidence.

It may be easiest for younger students to conduct interviews in small groups, with one note-taker using a clipboard, one recorder and one interviewer). At each interview, students should record the date and time, as well as the name, title and contact information of the person being interviewed. They should seek permission before taking photos or using a tape recorder. Remind students to thank the interviewee in person and promptly send a note of thanks. Discussing their interview with classmates will help students synthesize what they have learned (see Reflection ideas on pages 45).

Some projects can benefit from the broader group input offered by a focus group of people who have an interest or stake in the problem students are investigating. Focus groups meet on a single occasion for informal conversation about a specified topic. Students may want to share some of their findings, ask targeted questions about the problem, or get reactions to their ideas. The meeting should have an experienced facilitator and note-taker. Set clear objectives (and a time limit) for the focus group and communicate these clearly to participants. Providing incentives for participation (like food students have made) can help increase turnout.

Conducting Surveys

Surveys can be done in a variety of forms—in person, by phone, by mail, by e-mail, or online. Good surveys are difficult to create, so it may be helpful to have a community expert help students. Have students organize their questions ahead of time, limiting themselves to five or fewer. Once surveys are completed, tabulate the responses. This is a place to integrate the use of technology in the collection, analysis, and synthesis of the survey data. Can the information be graphed? Determine the best ways to present survey responses to other people.

Telephone Interview Form

When the person you want to speak with is on the telephone...

Identify yourself   Hello. This is _____ .

                                       From_____ School.

Why are you calling   I am calling to _____

_____

_____

_____

_____

_____

_____

_____

Are there questions?   Do you have any questions?

THANK YOU   Thank you for

                                       _____

Interview Form

Researching the Problem

Name/Names of Group Members:

Date:

Problem Statement:

Name of person interviewed:

The person's role in the community:

Tell the person about the problem you are studying.
Then ask the following questions:

▶ Do you think this problem is important? Why or why not?

▶ Do you think others in this community think this problem is important? Why?

▶ What are the causes of this problem?

▶ What are the effects of this problem? What individuals or groups are most affected by this problem?

▶ What is the community (government, business, nonprofit organizations) currently doing about this problem?

▶ Where can we go for more information about this problem and learn about the different positions that people have on this issue?

Adapted from Active Citizenship Today-Teacher Handbook, and from Project Citizen (see full references in Chapter 8).

Explore the Problem

Modes of research: *Guest speaker:* **GS**   *Interviews:* **I**   *Survey:* **S***
Primary materials: **PM**   *Secondary materials:* **SM**

*Surveys could be secondary (e.g., use of existing data) or primary (e.g., student-generated)

Problem:

History:
When did the problem start? How has it changed over time? How have people addressed this issue over time?

Causes:
What leads to this problem?
Claim (the idea) & evidence (the information that indicates something is true)

Claim:

Evidence:

Claim:

Evidence:

Claim:

Evidence:

Effects:
What impact is the problem having on people, property, environment, organizations, etc.?

Claim

Evidence:

Claim:

Evidence:

Claim:

Evidence:

Multiple Perspectives:
How do different people/groups view the problem? Do they agree or disagree about causes and effects?

Student Reflection on the Problem:

Ways to Approach a Problem

Objectives:
▶ Warm-up
▶ Introduce the different approaches to a service-learning problem
▶ Understand that there are multiple ways to solve a problem

Materials:
▶ Chart paper with problem and different approaches
▶ Tape
▶ Questions/prompts below

Process:
(In advance, tape three different approaches examples on walls - see page 61.)

1. Turn to page 61 and discuss the three different approaches.

2. Discuss problem that students are addressing on these charts.

3. Ask a few key questions (see below). Participants will go to the corner that best answers the question for them. Depending on time and facilitator and participant interests, ask one to five of these questions:
   • Which approach do you like the best? (Discuss why in the corner.)
   • What approach do you think students would like/have the most excitement for? (Why?)
   • Which approach would require the most research? (What would they need to research?)
   • Which would have the most impact? (Which would have the most long-term impact?)
   • Which one would require the most work?

4. Divide groups, if necessary, into three fairly equal groups, each in front of an approach wall sheet.

5. Ask them to think of solutions to a given problem (see exmples below) based on the approach that they are standing in front of. Then rotate to next two approaches.
   • We generate too much trash that goes to our landfill.
   • Too many children are overweight in this country.
   • Underage drinking is a growing problem.

Consider Potential Solutions

Chosen Problem/Need:

Approach	Potential Local Partners/Experts for Each Solution
1. Direct Approach:	
2. Educate Appropriate Community Members:	
3. Influence Decision Makers (Policy):	

Comparing Solutions

Brief description of proposed solution A:

Criteria	Advantages	Disadvantages
IMPACT		
FEASIBILITY		
NEW KNOWLEDGE & SKILLS		
CARE		
OTHER?		

Brief description of proposed solution B:

Criteria	Advantages	Disadvantages
IMPACT		
FEASIBILITY		
NEW KNOWLEDGE & SKILLS		
CARE		
OTHER?		

Decision-Making Matrix

Place criteria on the y-axis and list possible solutions on the x-axis. On a scale of 1-5 rate each solution for all criteria (with 1 being least and 5 being most effective):

	POSSIBLE SOLUTIONS			
Will proposed solution solve the problem?				
Is it feasible?				
Will we learn new knowledge and skills?				
Do we care about this?				
Total Points				

CRITERIA

Action Plan with Timeline

Objective	Tasks and Activities	Person Responsible	Completion Date	Status

Student Planning Sheet

Project name: _____

_____

Group name and members: _____

_____

_____

Group objective: _____

_____

_____

We will be assessed on: (product and process) _____

_____

_____

We will help the community by:_____

_____

_____

Tasks:

What?	Who?	By When?

What will we learn? (list subjects) _____

_____

What resources will we need? (materials, community members) _____

_____

_____

_____ _____ _____
Student   Parent   Administrator

Project Brief

First Name _____ Last Name _____

Position_____

Grade Level _____

Email _____

Phone Number_____ ext _____

School/Organization Name _____

Address_____

      City _____ State _____ Zip_____

Number of Students Involved_____

1. What community problem/need was addressed through this project?

2. How did studetns gauge the impact of their project on this problem/need?

3. Who were the community partners involved with students?

4. How did students demonstrate what they learned?

Completion Date_____

Students' Academic Reflections, or Other Comments/Notes

Community Partner Survey Form

Dear Community Partner:

Thank you for your participation in a service-learning project. Please take a moment to provide us with some feedback about your experience working with students and teachers in your community. Your responses will be used to help us measure the impact of service-learning in your community and improve the effectiveness of future school-community collaborations.

Name _____ Organization/Business _____

Position_____ School Partner_____

1. Please provide a brief description of the service-learning project with which you were involved.

2. What type(s) of assistance did you provide (please check all that apply):

   ❑ provided information about a community need or issue by phone/mail

   ❑ presented information about a community need or issue to students

   ❑ helped students with project design

   ❑ provided materials and/or supplies for the project

   ❑ helped students with project implementation

   ❑ other (please describe)

3. How would you rate the amount of time and effort that you put into this project?

1	2	3	4
none	a little	moderate	a great deal

3a. How satisfied were you with this level of involvement?

1	2	3
I would have liked to be more involved	This was the appropriate amount of involvement	This took too much time

4. What other types of community projects would be useful to your community?

Community Partner Survey Form (cont.)

5. Please read the statements below and circle the letters that best represent your opinion:
   KEY: **SA**=*Strongly Agree* **A**=*Agree* **D**=*Disagree* **SD**=*Strongly Disagree* **DK**=*Don't Know*

a. Real community needs were addressed by the project. COMMENTS:	SA	A	D	SD	DK
b. Projects like the one(s) that occurred in your community this past year improved community attitudes toward youth. COMMENTS:	SA	A	D	SD	DK
c. Projects like the one(s) that occurred in your community this past year improved schoolcommunity relationships. COMMENTS:	SA	A	D	SD	DK
d. Projects like the one(s) that occurred in your community this past year help to provide a meaningful role for youth in the community. COMMENTS:	SA	A	D	SD	DK
e. Projects like the one(s) that occurred in your community this past year reduce the at-risk behaviors of youth (e.g., substance abuse, teenage pregnancy, youth crime). COMMENTS:	SA	A	D	SD	DK
f. Projects like the one(s) that occurred in your community this past year help students understand how community decisions are made. COMMENTS:	SA	A	D	SD	DK
g. Projects like the one(s) that occurred in your community this past year help students understand the different kinds of services our community provides. COMMENTS:	SA	A	D	SD	DK
h. I believe that students can influence community decisions. COMMENTS:	SA	A	D	SD	DK
i. Overall, I was satisfied with how the project went. COMMENTS:	SA	A	D	SD	DK
j. If given a chance, I would be involved in a similar project again. COMMENTS:	SA	A	D	SD	DK

Thank you for your assistance!

KIDS Checklist for a Successful Service-Learning Project

✓=Strengths of your project;　　X=Areas that need work;　　n/a=Areas that don't apply

Academic Integrity

Does/Did this Project...

- [ ] have clear academic learning objectives
- [ ] meet the needs of all students
- [ ] place teachers in a facilitating role
- [ ] give all students an opportunity to demonstrate new knowledge
- [ ] incorporate assessment of student work
- [ ] motivate students
- [ ] engage students in regular reflection on their experiences (cognitive and affective)

Student Ownership

Does/Did this Project...

- [ ] include a strong student voice in project selection, planning and implementation
- [ ] provide students with opportunities to exercise their leadership and problem-solving skills
- [ ] have a clear plan and timeline
- [ ] teach students the skills necessary to succeed
- [ ] celebrate classroom progress
- [ ] allow students to take new challenges and risks
- [ ] encourage students and adults to be equal partners
- [ ] allow students to explore their strengths and set individual goals
- [ ] teach students that they have the power to make a difference

Apprentice Citizenship

Does/Did this Project...

- [ ] meet real community needs and/or solve community problems
- [ ] foster understanding of an issue through research and investigation
- [ ] have an authentic community audience that values students' work
- [ ] involve students in learning and working with community members
- [ ] help students to learn about and participate in their community and governance structures
- [ ] provide a tangible benefit for the community
- [ ] include multiple opportunities for students to share their project with others
- [ ] make students feel like they belong to a community

Assessing Your Service-Learning Practice

Using National K-12 Standards for Quality Service-Learning Practice

Service-learning actively engages participants in meaningful and personally relevant service activities.	**Meaningful Service** overall rating:	Weak	Needs Work	Strong
	1. Service-learning experiences are appropriate to participant ages and developmental abilities.			
	2. Service-learning addresses issues that are personally relevant to the participants.			
	3. Service-learning provides participants with interesting and engaging service activities.			
	4. Service-learning encourages participants to understand their service experiences in the context of the underlying societal issues being addressed.			
	5. Service-learning leads to attainable and visible outcomes that are valued by those being served.			
Service-learning provides youth with a strong voice in planning, implementing, and evaluating service-learning experiences with guidance from adults.	**Youth Voice** overall rating:	Weak	Needs Work	Strong
	1. Service-learning engages youth in generating ideas during the planning, implementation, and evaluation processes.			
	2. Service-learning involves youth in the decision-making process throughout the service-learning experience.			
	3. Service-learning involves youth and adults in creating an environment that supports trust and open expression of ideas.			
	4. Service-learning promotes acquisition of knowledge and skills to enhance youth leadership and decision-making.			
	5. Service-learning involves youth in evaluating the quality and effectiveness of the service-learning experience.			
Service-learning is intentionally used as an instructional strategy to meet learning goals and/or content standards.	**Link to Curriculum** overall rating:	Weak	Needs Work	Strong
	1. Service-learning has clearly articulated learning goals.			
	2. Service-learning is aligned with the academic and/or programmatic curriculum.			
	3. Service-learning helps participants learn how to transfer knowledge and skills from one setting to another.			
	4. Service-learning that takes place in schools is formally recognized in school board policies and student records.			
Service-learning incorporates multiple challenging reflection activities that are ongoing and that prompt deep thinking and analysis about oneself and one's relationship to society.	**Reflection** overall rating:	Weak	Needs Work	Strong
	1. Service-learning reflection includes a variety of verbal, written, artistic, and nonverbal activities to demonstrate understanding and changes in participants' knowledge, skills, and/or attitudes.			
	2. Service-learning reflection occurs before, during, and after the service experience.			
	3. Service-learning reflection prompts participants to think deeply about complex community problems and alternative solutions.			
	4. Service-learning reflection encourages participants to examine their preconceptions and assumptions in order to explore and understand their roles and responsibilities as citizens.			
	5. Service-learning reflection encourages participants to examine a variety of social and civic issues related to their service-learning experience so that participants understand connections to public policy and civic life.			

Adapted from *Assessing and Improving Your Service-Learning Practice*, Institute for Global Education and Service-Learning, 2008

Assessing Your Service-Learning Practice (cont.)

Using National K-12 Standards for Quality Service-Learning Practice

	Partnerships overall rating:	Weak	Needs Work	Strong
Service-learning partnerships are collaborative, mutually beneficial, and address community needs.	1. Service-learning involves a variety of partners, including, youth, educators, families, community members, community-based organizations, and/or businesses.			
	2. Service-learning partnerships are characterized by frequent and regular communication to keep all partners well-informed about activities and progress.			
	3. Service-learning partners collaborate to establish a shared vision and set common goals to address community needs.			
	4. Service-learning partners collaboratively develop and implement action plans to meet specified goals.			
	5. Service-learning partners share knowledge and understanding of school and community assets and needs, and view each other as valued resources.			
	Diversity overall rating:	Weak	Needs Work	Strong
Service-learning promotes understanding of diversity and mutual respect among all participants.	1. Service-learning helps participants identify and analyze different points of view to gain understanding of multiple perspectives.			
	2. Service-learning helps participants develop interpersonal skills in conflict resolution and group decision-making.			
	3. Service-learning helps participants actively seek to understand and value the diverse backgrounds and perspectives of those offering and receiving service.			
	4. Service-learning encourages participants to recognize and overcome stereotypes.			
	Progress Monitoring overall rating:	Weak	Needs Work	Strong
Service-learning engages participants in an ongoing process to assess the quality of implementation and progress toward meeting specified goals, and uses results for improvement and sustainability.	1. Service-learning participants collect evidence of progress toward meeting specific goals and learning outcomes from multiple sources throughout the service-learning experience.			
	2. Service-learning participants collect evidence of the quality of service-learning implementation from multiple sources throughout the service-learning experience.			
	3. Service-learning participants use evidence to improve service-learning experiences.			
	4. Service-learning participants communicate evidence of progress toward goals and outcomes with the broader community, including policy-makers and education leaders, to deepen service-learning understanding and ensure that high quality practices are sustained.			
	Duration & Intensity overall rating:	Weak	Needs Work	Strong
Service-learning has sufficient duration and intensity to address community needs and meet specified outcomes.	1. Service-learning experiences include the processes of investigating community needs, preparing for service, action, reflection, demonstration of learning and impact, and celebration.			
	2. Service-learning is conducted during concentrated blocks of time across a period of several weeks or months.			
	3. Service-learning experiences provide enough time to address identified community needs and achieve learning results.			

Adapted from *Assessing and Improving Your Service-Learning Practice*, Institute for Global Education and Service-Learning, 2008